UNL⌀CK

LISTENING & SPEAKING SKILLS 3

Matt Firth

CAMBRIDGE
UNIVERSITY PRESS

CAMBRIDGE
UNIVERSITY PRESS

University Printing House, Cambridge CB2 8BS, United Kingdom

Cambridge University Press is part of the University of Cambridge.

It furthers the University's mission by disseminating knowledge in the pursuit of education, learning and research at the highest international levels of excellence.

www.cambridge.org
Information on this title: www.cambridge.org/9781107681545

© Cambridge University Press 2014

Content and images which are © Discovery Communications, LLC are reproduced here under license.

First published 2014
Reprinted 2014

Printed in the United Kingdom by Latimer Trend

A catalogue record for this publication is available from the British Library

ISBN 978-1-107-68728-8 Listening and Speaking Student's Book 3 with Online Workbook
ISBN 978-1-107-68154-5 Listening and Speaking Teacher's Book 3 with DVD
ISBN 978-1-107-61526-7 Reading and Writing Student's Book 3 with Online Workbook
ISBN 978-1-107-61404-8 Reading and Writing Teacher's Book 3 with DVD

Additional resources for this publication at www.cambridge.org/unlock

CONTENTS

UNLOCK UNIT STRUCTURE

The units in *Unlock Listening and Speaking Skills* are carefully scaffolded so that students build the skills and language they need throughout the unit in order to produce a successful Speaking task.

UNLOCK YOUR KNOWLEDGE	Encourages discussion around the theme of the unit with inspiration from interesting questions and striking visuals.
WATCH AND LISTEN	Features an engaging and motivating *Discovery Education*™ video which generates interest in the topic.
LISTENING 1	Provides information about the topic and practises pre-listening, while listening and post-listening skills. This section also includes a focus on a pronunciation feature which will further enhance listening comprehension.
LANGUAGE DEVELOPMENT	Practises the vocabulary and grammar from Listening 1 and pre-teaches the vocabulary and grammar from Listening 2.
LISTENING 2	Provides a different angle on the topic and serves as a model for the speaking task.
CRITICAL THINKING	Contains brainstorming, categorizing, evaluative and analytical tasks as preparation for the speaking task.
PREPARATION FOR SPEAKING / SPEAKING SKILLS	Presents and practises functional language, pronunciation and speaking strategies for the speaking task.
SPEAKING TASK	Uses the skills and strategies learnt over the course of the unit to produce a presentational or interactional speaking task.
OBJECTIVES REVIEW	Allows learners to assess how well they have mastered the skills covered in the unit.
WORDLIST	Includes the key vocabulary from the unit.

This is the unit's main learning objective. It gives learners the opportunity to use all the language and skills they have learnt in the unit.

UNL⌀CK MOTIVATION

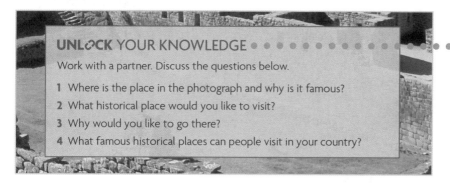

UNL⌀CK YOUR KNOWLEDGE

Work with a partner. Discuss the questions below.

1 Where is the place in the photograph and why is it famous?
2 What historical place would you like to visit?
3 Why would you like to go there?
4 What famous historical places can people visit in your country?

PERSONALIZE

Unlock encourages students to bring their own knowledge, experiences and opinions to the topics. This **motivates** students to relate the topics to their own contexts.

DISCOVERY EDUCATION™ VIDEO

Thought-provoking videos from *Discovery Education™* are included in every unit throughout the course to introduce topics, promote discussion and motivate learners. The videos provide a new angle on a wide range of academic subjects.

" The video was excellent! It helped with raising students' interest in the topic. It was well-structured and the language level was appropriate.

Maria Agata Szczerbik,
United Arab Emirates University,
Al-Ain, UAE "

UNL⊘CK CRITICAL THINKING

> [...] with different styles of visual aids such as mind maps, grids, tables and pictures, this [critical thinking] section [provides] very crucial tools that can encourage learners to develop their speaking skills.
>
> Dr. Panidnad Chulerk, Rangit University, Thailand

BLOOM'S TAXONOMY

CREATE — create, invent, plan, compose, construct, design, imagine

EVALUATE — decide, rate, choose, recommend, justify, assess, prioritize

ANALYZE — explain, contrast, examine, identify, investigate, categorize

APPLY — show, complete, use, classify, examine, illustrate, solve

UNDERSTAND — compare, discuss, restate, predict, translate, outline

REMEMBER — name, describe, relate, find, list, write, tell

BLOOM'S TAXONOMY

The Critical thinking sections in *Unlock* are based on Benjamin Bloom's classification of learning objectives. This ensures learners develop their **lower-** and **higher-order thinking skills**, ranging from demonstrating **knowledge** and **understanding** to in-depth **evaluation**.
The margin headings in the Critical thinking sections highlight the exercises which develop Bloom's concepts.

LEARN TO THINK

Learners engage in **evaluative** and **analytical tasks** that are designed to ensure they do all of the thinking and information-gathering required for the end-of-unit speaking task.

CRITICAL THINKING

At the end of this unit you are going to do the speaking task below.

> How has modern technology changed the way we interact with each other? What are the positive and negative aspects of this influence?

UNDERSTAND

1 Look at the ideas map. What is the main focus?

clicking on like — *sending greetings* — *playing games* — **social-networking activities** — *commenting on photos* — *posting profile updates*

2 Work with a partner. Add extra examples to the ideas map.

3 Work with another pair. Take turns to explain your extra examples.

UNL⌀CK RESEARCH

THE CAMBRIDGE LEARNER CORPUS ⊙

The **Cambridge Learner Corpus** is a bank of official Cambridge English exam papers. Our exclusive access means we can use the corpus to carry out unique research and identify the most common errors that learners make. That information is used to ensure the *Unlock* syllabus teaches the most **relevant language**.

THE WORDS YOU NEED

Language Development sections provide vocabulary and grammar-building tasks that are further practised in the **UNL⌀CK ONLINE** Workbook. The glossary provides definitions and pronunciation, and the end-of-unit wordlists provide useful summaries of key vocabulary.

⊙ LANGUAGE DEVELOPMENT · · · · · · · · · · UNL⌀CK ONLINE · · · · · · ·

Word families

You can develop your academic vocabulary by working on word families. When you record a new word in your notebook, make sure to write down any other forms from its word family.

1 Complete the table below. Sometimes there is more than one possible answer. Use a dictionary to help you.

noun	verb	adjective	adverb

PRONUNCIATION FOR LISTENING · · · · · · · · · · UNL⌀CK ONLINE · · · · · ·

Connected speech: weak forms

When we speak fluently, some words are not usually pronounced in a strong or clear way. These are usually auxiliary verbs (*has, was, do,* etc.), modals (*would, can,* etc.), prepositions (*to, for,* etc.) and other small words (*and, you,* etc.).

When small words are not pronounced clearly, we call this a 'weak form'. These words are pronounced with a /ə/ sound.

4 🔊 3.2 Listen to extracts from the discussion. Notice the pronunciation of the highlighted words.

1 Has the professor sent us the list of possible topics to choose from?
2 OK, we can do that.
3 Some of them are human and some are animals.

ACADEMIC LANGUAGE

Unique research using the **Cambridge English Corpus** has been carried out into academic language, in order to provide learners with relevant, academic vocabulary from the start (CEFR A1 and above). This addresses a gap in current academic vocabulary mapping and ensures learners are presented with carefully selected words which they will find essential during their studies.

PRONUNCIATION FOR LISTENING

This unique feature of *Unlock* focuses on aspects of pronunciation which may inhibit listening comprehension. This means that learners are primed to understand detail and nuance while listening.

" The language development is clear and the strong lexical focus is positive as learners feel they make more progress when they learn more vocabulary.
Colleen Wackrow,
Princess Nourah Bint Abdulrahman University, Al-Riyadh, Kingdom of Saudi Arabia "

UNL❂CK SOLUTIONS

FLEXIBLE

Unlock is available in a range of print and digital components, so teachers can mix and match according to their requirements.

UNL❂CK ONLINE WORKBOOKS

The **UNL❂CK ONLINE** Workbooks are accessed via activation codes packaged with the Student's Books. These **easy-to-use** workbooks provide interactive exercises, games, tasks, and further practice of the language and skills from the Student's Books in the Cambridge LMS, an engaging and modern learning environment.

CAMBRIDGE LEARNING MANAGEMENT SYSTEM (LMS)

The Cambridge LMS provides teachers with the ability to track learner progress and save valuable time thanks to automated marking functionality. Blogs, forums and other tools are also available to facilitate communication between students and teachers.

UNL❂CK EBOOKS

The *Unlock* Student's Books and Teacher's Books are also available as interactive eBooks. With answers and *Discovery Education™* videos embedded, the eBooks provide a great alternative to the printed materials.

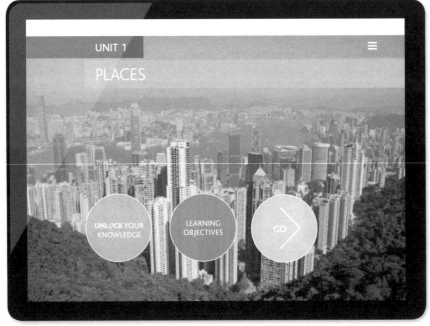

1 Using video in the classroom

The *Watch and listen* sections in *Unlock* are based on documentary-style videos from *Discovery Education*™. Each one provides a fresh angle on the unit topic and a stimulating lead-in to the unit.

There are many different ways of using the video in class. For example, you could ask learners to listen to the audio track of the video without viewing the images and ask learners what the video is about. Then show the whole video and check whether the learners were correct. You could ask learners to reconstruct the voiceover or record their own commentary to the video. Try not to interrupt the first viewing of a new video, you can go back and watch sections again or explain things for struggling learners. You can also watch with the subtitles turned on when the learners have done all the listening comprehension work required of them. For less-controlled listening practice, use the video for free note-taking and ask learners to compare their notes to the video script.

See also: Goldstein, B. and Driver, P. (2014) *Language Learning with Digital Video*, Cambridge University Press, and the *Unlock* website www.cambridge.org/unlock for more ideas on using video in the classroom.

2 Teaching listening skills

Learners who aim to study at university will need to be comfortable listening to long, complex listening texts in a number of different genres. The listening texts in *Unlock Listening & Speaking Skills* provide learners with practice in the different listening sub-skills and also provide topic-related ideas and functional language needed for the *Speaking task*. Every unit focuses on one key listening skill, which is highlighted in a box, as well as various sub-skills so that learners build on their listening skills throughout.

Before listening for the first time, use the *Preparing to listen* skills boxes to draw on learners' background knowledge and expectations of the listening text. Use the *While listening* skills boxes to focus students on listening sub-skills. Use the *Pronunciation for listening* activities to raise awareness of pronunciation features which can help listeners decode speech. Learners have an opportunity

for reflection on what they have listened to in the *Discussion* activities.

3 Teaching pronunciation

Unlock features *Pronunciation for listening* and *Pronunciation for speaking* sections. In *Pronunciation for listening*, learners focus on aspects of pronunciation which can enhance their listening comprehension, such as linking words, intonation, strong and weak forms in connected speech, homophones, etc. This will help learners to obtain more meaning from the listening text and in real life. Encourage learners to try using these pronunciation features in their own speaking so that they will be primed to hear them.

In *Pronunciation for speaking*, learners focus on aspects of pronunciation which they can put into practice in the *Speaking task*, such as consonant clusters, vowel sounds, connected speech, sentence stress and using intonation and tone. Practise pronunciation with your learners by recording them and giving feedback on the clarity, pace and stress in the *Speaking task*. Encourage your learners to record themselves and reflect on their own pronunciation.

4 Teaching speaking skills

Learners work towards the *Speaking task* throughout the unit by learning vocabulary and grammar relevant for the task, and then by listening to the key issues involved in the topic. Learners gather, organize and evaluate this information in the *Critical thinking* section and use it to prepare the *Speaking task*. *Unlock* includes two types of *Speaking task* – presentational and interactional. In the presentational tasks, learners will be required to give a presentation or monologue about the topic, often as part of a team. The interactional tasks require learners to role-play or interact with another person or persons.

There is an *Additional speaking task* for every unit in the Teacher's Book. This can be used as extra speaking practice to be prepared at home and done in class or as part of an end-of-unit test/evaluation. The *Additional speaking task* is also available on the Online Workbook. See section 8 for more details.

If your learners require IELTS test practice, point out that the discussion questions in the *Unlock your knowledge* sections provide practice of *IELTS Part 1 and 3* and the *Speaking tasks* provide practice of *IELTS Part 2*. Set the *Speaking task* as a timed test with a minimum time of two minutes and grade the learners on their overall fluency, vocabulary and grammar and the quality and clarity of their pronunciation.

5 Managing discussions in the classroom

There are opportunities for free discussion throughout *Unlock Listening & Speaking Skills*. The photographs and the *Unlock your knowledge* boxes on the first page of each unit provide the first discussion opportunity. Learners could be asked to guess what is happening in the photographs or predict what is going to happen or they could investigate the questions for homework in preparation for the lesson.

Throughout the rest of the unit, the heading *Discussion* indicates a set of questions which can be an opportunity for free speaking practice. Learners can use these questions to develop their ideas about the topic and gain confidence in the arguments they will put forward in the *Speaking task*.

To maximize speaking practice, learners could complete the discussion sections in pairs. Monitor each pair to check they can find enough to say and help where necessary. Encourage learners to minimize their use of L1 (their first language) and make notes of any error correction and feedback after the learners have finished speaking.

An alternative approach might be to ask learners to role-play discussions in the character of one of the people in the unit. This may free the learners from the responsibility to provide the correct answer and allow them to see an argument from another perspective.

• Task checklists

Encourage your learners to reflect on their performance in the *Speaking task* by referring to the *Task checklist* at the end of the unit. The checklists can also be used by learners to reflect on each other's performance, if you feel that your learners will be comfortable doing so.

• Additional speaking tasks

There are ten Additional speaking tasks in the Teacher's Book, one for each unit. These provide another opportunity to practise the skills and language learnt in the unit.

• Model language

Model language in the form of functional expressions and conversation gambits follow the *Additional speaking tasks* to help learners develop confidence in their speaking ability by providing chunks of language they can use during the *Speaking task*. Photocopy the *Model language* and hand this to your learners when they plan and perform their writing task. Make sure learners practise saying them before they begin their task.

6 Teaching vocabulary

The *Wordlist* at the end of each unit includes topic vocabulary and academic vocabulary. There are many ways that you can work with the vocabulary. During the early units, encourage the learners to learn the new words by setting regular review tests. You could ask the learners to choose, e.g. five words from the unit vocabulary to learn. Encourage your learners to keep a vocabulary notebook and use new words as much as possible in their speaking.

7 Using the Research projects with your class

There is an opportunity for students to investigate and explore the unit topic further in the *Research projects* which feature at the end of each unit in the Teacher's Books. These are optional activities which will allow your learners to work in groups (or individually) to discover more about a particular aspect of the topic, carry out a problem-solving activity or engage in a task which takes their learning outside the classroom.

Learners can make use of the Cambridge LMS tools to share their work with the teacher or with the class as a whole. See section 8 for more ideas.

8 Using UNL✷CK digital components: Online Workbook and the Cambridge Learning Management System (LMS)

The Online Workbook provides:

- additional practice of the key skills and language covered in the Student's Book through interactive exercises. The **UNLOCK ONLINE** symbol next to a section or activity in the Student's Book means that there is additional practice of that language or skill in the Online Workbook. These exercises are ideal as homework.

- *Additional speaking tasks* from the Teacher's Books. You can ask your learners to carry out the *Additional speaking tasks* in the

Online Workbook for homework. Learners can record their response to the task and upload the file for the teacher.

- a gradebook which allows you to track your learners' progress throughout the course. This can help structure a one-to-one review with the learner or be used as a record of learning. You can also use this to help you decide what to review in class.
- games for vocabulary and language practice which are not scored in the gradebook.

The Cambridge LMS provides the following tools:

• Blogs

The class blog can be used for free writing practice to consolidate learning and share ideas. For example, you could ask each learner to post a description of their holiday (or another event linked to a topic covered in class). You could ask them to read and comment on two other learners' posts.

• Forums

The forums can be used for discussions. You could post a discussion question and encourage learners to post their thoughts on the question for homework.

• Wikis

In each class there is a Wiki. You can set up pages within this. The wikis are ideal for whole-class project work. You can use the wiki to practise process writing and to train the students to redraft and proofread. Try not to correct students online. Take note of common errors and use these to create a fun activity to review the language in class.

See www.cambridge.org/unlock for more ideas on using these tools with your class.

How to access the Cambridge LMS and setup classes

Go to www.cambridge.org/unlock for more information for teachers on accessing and using the Cambridge LMS and Online Workbooks.

---

9 Using Unlock interactive eBooks

Unlock Listening & Speaking Skills Student's Books are available as fully interactive eBooks. The content of the printed Student's Book and the Student's eBook is the same. However, there will be a number of differences in the way some content appears.

If you are using the interactive eBooks on tablet devices in the classroom, you may want to consider how this affects your class structure. For example, your learners will be able to independently access the video and audio content via the eBook. This means learners could do video activities at home and class time could be optimized on discussion activities and other productive tasks. Learners can compare their responses to the answer key in their eBooks which means the teacher may need to spend less time on checking answers with the whole class, leaving more time to monitor learner progress and help individual learners.

10 Using mobile technology in the language learning classroom

By Michael Pazinas, Curriculum and assessment coordinator for the Foundation Program at the United Arab Emirates University.

The presiding learning paradigm for mobile technology in the language classroom should be to create as many meaningful learning opportunities as possible for its users. What should be at the core of this thinking is that while modern mobile technology can be a 21st century 'super-toolbox', it should be there to support a larger learning strategy. Physical and virtual learning spaces, content and pedagogy all need to be factored in before deciding on delivery and ultimately the technological tools needed.

It is with these factors in mind that the research projects featured in this Teacher's Book aim to add elements of hands-on enquiry, collaboration, critical thinking and analysis. They have real challenges, which learners have to research and find solutions for. In an ideal world, they can become tangible, important solutions. While they are designed with groups in mind, there is nothing to stop them being used with individuals. They can be fully enriching experiences, used as starting points or simply ideas to be adapted and streamlined. When used in these ways, learner devices can become research libraries, film, art and music studios, podcast stations, marketing offices and blog creation tools.

Michael has first-hand experience of developing materials for the paperless classroom. He is the author of the Research projects *which feature in the Teacher's Books.*

1 ANIMALS

Learning objectives

Before you start the *Unlock your knowledge* section, ask students to read the Learning objectives box. This will give them a clear idea of what they will learn in the unit. Tell them that you will return to these objectives at the end of the unit, when they review what they have learned. Give students the opportunity to ask any questions they might have.

UNLOCK YOUR KNOWLEDGE

Background note

The photo shows animals working. In this picture, a team of dogs are pulling the sledge. This particular breed of dog is called a husky, and they are very fast and powerful. They are found in the arctic, in regions such as Alaska, Canada, Scandinavia and Russia.

1 Students discuss the questions in pairs. Allow a minute for discussion, before inviting feedback the class.

> #### Possible answers
>
> The dogs are huskies. Their job is to pull sledges in northern regions, such as Alaska, Scandinavia or Russia.

2 Ask the students to work together in pairs or small groups and think of other working animals and the types of task these animals perform. Allow 3–4 minutes for discussion and then invite feedback from the class. During the feedback, you could also ask the class which one animal they think can perform the greatest number of tasks.

> #### Possible answers
>
> Answers will vary, but examples of working animals include hunting, herding sheep, guiding the blind, carrying things and searching for people.

3 If your class are mostly from the same country, quickly elicit ideas from the whole group. If you have students from a number of different countries or regions, ask them to form small groups with at least two different nationalities in each group. Allow up to two minutes for discussion, then invite feedback from the class.

WATCH AND LISTEN

Video script

This is the South African savannah: a huge open area of grassland in the east of the country. Warm air from the Indian Ocean brings plenty of rainfall and a land full of life.

Here you will find lions and rhinos, zebras, elephants and giraffes, and a South African gazelle called the springbok, all living in one of the world's great natural wildlife parks.

Wildlife vets like Jana Pretorius work hard to protect South Africa's animal species. Jana moves 6,000 animals across the country each year, taking them back to places where they used to live and helping to increase the population.

It is thanks to people like Jana that South Africa leads the world in wildlife conservation, with 10% of the country set aside for the protection of wildlife. Today, Jana and her team have to find, capture, and relocate a male giraffe which is five and a half metres tall.

Jana flies over the savannah in a helicopter, searching for the giraffe. The helicopter flies low over the trees, travelling at 160 kilometres an hour. When Jana finds the giraffe she will have to shoot it with a sedative dart. The sedative is very strong. One teaspoon of it would kill 25 people.

On the ground, Jana's team travel in trucks. It is their job to control the giraffe after Jana has sedated it. This is very dangerous work. It takes Jana an hour to find the giraffe herd. She isolates the tallest male and shoots him with the sedative dart.

The team need to get to the giraffe and keep it in the open. If Jana doesn't give the giraffe the antidote quickly enough, it will die.

Everything goes well. Jana wakes the giraffe up and the team gets the animal on the truck. It will now travel 800 kilometres to its new home, while Jana flies off to her next job.

PREPARING TO WATCH
UNDERSTANDING KEY VOCABULARY

1 Give students one minute to read the information and be ready to explain what the organization does. Elicit a brief explanation from one of the students. With a stronger class, you could ask the students to read through the text and pay special attention to the words in bold. With a partner, they should then take it in turns to try and explain the meanings of the bolded words.

2 Allow the students two minutes to match the words with the definitions either individually or with a partner (stronger students may need less time).

| Answers
1 herd 2 capture 3 wildlife conservation 4 sedate
5 savannah 6 relocate

WHILE WATCHING
UNDERSTANDING MAIN IDEAS

3 Students watch the video and decide which animals are mentioned.

| Answers
lions, rhinos, zebras, elephants, giraffes and gazelles

4 Ask the class to read the three captions for each photo and to decide with a partner which are the best. Then play the video a second time and ask the students to check their answers. Elicit the answers from the class.

| Answers
1 b 2 a 3 b 4 c

UNDERSTANDING DETAIL

5 Ask students to read statements 1–8 first, and decide whether they might be true or false. Then play the video again for them to check their answers.

| Answers
1 T 2 T 3 F 4 T 5 T 6 F 7 F 8 F

DISCUSSION

6 Students discuss the questions in pairs. Allow 3–5 minutes for discussion, then quickly elicit two or three ideas for each of the four questions from the class.

LISTENING 1

Optional activity

Students often like discussing TV programmes they remember from their childhood, and this provides a good opportunity to personalize the next section. Ask students to think of some TV programmes they remember from their childhood that involved animals. In groups of three, the students should take it in turns to describe one of the TV programmes they thought of, but not to say its name. The other students should try and guess the name of the programme. Allow up to five minutes for the discussion, then quickly elicit the names of all of the TV programmes described from the class.

PREPARING TO LISTEN
UNDERSTANDING KEY VOCABULARY

1 Give the students three minutes to complete the task individually and then check their answers in pairs. Quickly go through the answers with the class.

| Answers
b lab
c take care of
d vets
e feed
f poisonous
g emergencies
h specialization
i results
j harmless

USING VISUALS TO PREDICT CONTENT

2 Allow a minute for the students to complete the task individually. Elicit suggestions from the class, but do not feed back at this point.

3 ◀) 1.1 Students complete the task individually. Quickly elicit the answers from the class.

| Answers
1 c 2 b 3 a

PRONUNCIATION FOR LISTENING

Language note

We use a special intonation pattern when reading out items in a list. Each item has a rising tone until the final item. The final item has a falling tone. This indicates to the listener that the list is finished. Examples of this are given in the next listening task. However, do not be surprised if some students find the differences in intonation hard to distinguish. Some people find it difficult to detect differences in intonation (listening in their own, or in a second language).

4 (◀) **1.2** 👤👥 Tell the students that they are going to hear two clips from a radio programme, and that their task is to listen carefully to the intonation of the lists. First, ask the students to read the extracts and the rules so that they know exactly what they have to do.

Play the recording once and ask students to quickly compare ideas with a partner. Then, play the recording again and tell the students to check their answers. Elicit the completed rules from the class.

Answers

1 The speaker pauses between each animal in the list, and stresses each word. In this example, the last word in the list has rising intonation. This means that the speaker thinks this **is not** a complete list
2 The speaker pauses between each activity in the list. In this example, the **last** activity has falling intonation. This means that the speaker **doesn't want** to add more examples and the list is **finished**.

5 (◀) **1.2** 👥 Play the recording again and ask students to repeat the sentences. Allow 1–2 minutes and carefully monitor the students to check that each pair is using the appropriate intonation pattern.

Optional activity

👥 Write the names of five types of food that you like on the board (e.g. *bananas, grapes, cheese, coffee, cakes* – any five will do). Call on one student to read the list out. Give feedback on the student's intonation. Next, ask each student to write their own list of five items personal to them. You could give examples, such as *favourite songs, countries I have visited, food I don't like*, etc. In pairs, the students read out their lists. Finish off by inviting some of the students to read their lists out to the class.

WHILE LISTENING

LISTENING FOR DETAIL

Optional activity

Ask the students to read the box on taking notes. If you feel comfortable talking about yourself in class, choose a topic that might interest your students based on one aspect of your life (e.g. *How I became a teacher / My first job / My studies*, etc.). Tell the students that you are going to talk about the topic for two minutes and that they should take notes. Give an informal talk, then ask the students to compare their notes in small groups. During their discussions, they should focus on similarities and differences in their note-taking style. For example, did they write full sentences? Did they use any abbreviations?

6 (◀) **1.3** 👥👥 Ask the students to read through the notes first. Then, play the recording and ask the students to complete the notes.

Answers

Specializations
1 **small animals**
2 **large animals**
3 exotic animals
Vet studies
1st & 2nd yr. **basic sciences**
3rd yr. **lab work**
4th yr. **work with a vet**
Emergencies
• food poisoning, e.g. **chocolate** can poison cats & dogs
• **snake bites**

Tips for vet sts.
• think about it **carefully**
• **get experience** e.g. animal shelter, zoo, etc.

7 👤👥 Teach the word *abbreviation* (= the short form of a longer word or phrase). Students complete the task individually or in pairs. Quickly go through the answers with the class.

Answers

1 e
2 d (*e.g.* is an abbreviation of the Latin phrase *exempli gratia*)
3 b
4 c (= and so on)
5 a (the symbol & is called an *ampersand*. It is based on a joining of the letters *e* and *t*, which spell *et*, the Latin word for *and*.)

POST-LISTENING

8 👤👥 Give the students up to two minutes to complete the task individually or in pairs. Quickly go through the answers with the class.

> **Answers**
> 1 b 2 a 3 b 4 b

DISCUSSION

9 Give the students 3–5 minutes to discuss the questions in small groups, then elicit one or two ideas for each question from the class.

⊙ LANGUAGE DEVELOPMENT

WORD FAMILIES

> **Optional activity**
>
> Ask the students to read the explanation box and to quickly look through the table below. Ask them if they notice anything about some of the parts of speech (the noun / verb / adjectival / adverbial form of each word). Elicit the fact not all word families have parts of speech for each word, and that there are sometimes more than one noun form and more than one adjectival form. Point out that it is useful to note down the different parts of speech, and that it is also important to know how to use these words. Elicit other ways of recording vocabulary effectively. One example would be to write down the words in a sentence that illustrates the meaning, or that contrasts the meanings of, for example, two different noun forms: *The continued **survival** of the **survivors** depends on how quickly the emergency services are able to reach them.* You could point out that while it may seem like a great deal of effort to write down an example sentence for each word, the students can easily find good examples online and simply copy and paste these into their smartphone notepad (or similar device).

1 👤👥 Give the students up to 10 minutes to complete the task individually or in pairs. Remind them that they can use dictionaries, and point out that many good dictionaries are available for free online (for example, by typing *Cambridge dictionary* into a search engine). If some students finish early, ask them to either go online and find examples of these words in use, or to write down sentences of their own illustrating the use of the words. Elicit answers from the class. If any students have written example sentences, elicit examples of these and comment as appropriate.

> **Answers**

noun	verb	adjective	adverb
abandonment	abandon	abandoned	
abuse	abuse	abused / abusive	abusively
analysis	analyze	analytical	analytically
benefit / benefactor / beneficiary	benefit	beneficial	beneficially
communication	communicate	communicated / communicative	communicatively
debate	debate	debated / debating / debateable	debatably
	domesticate	domesticated / domestic	domestically
environment		environmental	environmentally
involvement	involve	involved	
survivor / survival	survive	survivable / surviving	
treatment	treat	treatable / treated	

2 👤 Give the students 5–10 minutes to complete the task individually and then check their answers with a partner. Go through the answers with the class.

> **Answers**
> 2 Domestic/Domesticated; survive
> 3 abandon
> 4 treatment
> 5 environmental
> 6 communicate
> 7 involved
> 8 beneficial
> 9 debate
> 10 abusive

MODALS FOR OBLIGATION AND SUGGESTIONS

3 👤 Ask the students to read the information in the box and to complete the task individually. Give the students up to two minutes, then elicit the answers from the class.

> **Answers**
> 1 obligation
> 2 recommendation
> 3 obligation
> 4 recommendation

4 👤 Give the students two minutes to complete the task individually and then check their answers with a partner.

> **Answers**
> - We can use _need to_, _have to_, _must_ and _have got to_ to express obligation. This means things that you believe are important and necessary, or the things that are required by a school or a formal authority.
> - We can use _should_, _shouldn't_ and _ought to_ to make a recommendation.

5 👥 Ask students to complete the task in pairs.

> **Answers**
> 1 a 2 a 3 b 4 a

LISTENING 2

PREPARING TO LISTEN
UNDERSTANDING KEY VOCABULARY

1 👤👥 Challenge the students to complete the task in under one minute.

> **Answers**
> 1 c 2 b 3 e 4 i 5 g 6 h 7 d 8 f 9 a

2 👤👥 Challenge the students to complete the task in under three minutes (two minutes in the case of a stronger class).

> **Answers**
> 1 Zoology   5 conditions
> 2 protect   6 issue
> 3 humane   7 domesticated
> 4 suffer   8 search

PREDICTING CONTENT

3 👥👥👥 Elicit one reason in favour of using animals for work and one reason against from the class. Then give the students four minutes to list as many reasons for or against as they can. Go through the answers with the class. Begin by calling on the student sitting furthest away from you to give one reason for using animals for work, then quickly ask each student in turn to give a different idea until all ideas are exhausted. Repeat the same procedure for question 2. Finish off by getting a show of hands of those in favour and those against.

4 🔊 1.4 👤 Students complete the exercise and check which of the ideas suggested during the class feedback session for Exercise 3 are mentioned.

WHILE LISTENING
LISTENING FOR MAIN IDEAS

5 🔊 1.4 👤👥 Play the recording again. Students complete the task individually and then check their answers with a partner. You could ask them to try and complete the table using their own ideas and what they remember from the first playing of the recording. Then, they check their answers during the second playing. Go through the answers with the class.

> **Answers**
>
> | | protection | building | transport | war |
> |----------|:----------:|:--------:|:---------:|:---:|
> | dogs | ✓ | | ✓ | |
> | horses | | ✓ | ✓ | ✓ |
> | elephants| | ✓ | ✓ | ✓ |
> | camels | | | ✓ | ✓ |

LISTENING FOR OPINION

6 🔊 1.4 👥 Ask students to discuss the possible answers to questions 1–6 in pairs. Then play the recording a third time and ask the students to complete the task in pairs.

> **Answers**
> 1 A 2 K 3 A 4 K 5 K 6 A

POST-LISTENING
CONTRASTING IDEAS

> **Language note**
>
> We use linkers (_but, yet, on the contrary, even though, however_, etc.) to contrast ideas and help the audience understand our point of view.

7 👤 Ask the students to complete the extracts. Go through the answers with the class.

> **Answers**
> 1 Yet / But / However
> 2 Yet / But / However
> 3 Even though
> 4 On the contrary

8 👤👥 Students complete the task individually and then check their answers with a partner. Go through the answers with the class.

> **Answers**
>
> 1 Even though 2 On the contrary 3 Yet
> 4 Even though 5 Yet

DISCUSSION

9 👤 Give students three minutes to complete the task individually in preparation for Exercise 10.

10 👥 Give the students five minutes to discuss their ideas in small groups, and tell each group to be ready to provide a brief summary of the arguments put forward. Then ask the first group to summarize their discussion. Ask each group in turn if they have anything to add that hasn't already been said.

CRITICAL THINKING

APPLY

1 👥 Students read the introduction to this section. Then put them into small groups and ask them to see how many places and situations they can list in two minutes. One person in each group should act as secretary. After two minutes, tell the secretaries to put their pens down and find out which group has the most ideas. Ask that group to present their ideas, then elicit any other suggestions from the rest of the class.

> **Possible answers**
>
> Answers may include circuses, zoos, animal shows, safaris, tourism, and animals used in television and film.

2 👥 Ask students to read the question, then lead a class discussion on the problems faced by working animals. Keep the discussion fairly fast paced, bringing it to a conclusion when ideas start to run out.

3 👤👥 Students complete the task individually or in pairs. Allow 2–3 minutes, then go through the answers with the class.

> **Answers**
>
> 1 against 2 for 3 against 4 for 5 for
> 6 against 7 for 8 against

CREATE

4 👥 Students complete the task in pairs. Tell them that they should find examples to support the arguments made in Exercise 3, not arguments to support their own ideas. Allow up to five minutes for students to think of an example for each argument, then elicit ideas for each from the class.

SPEAKING

PREPARATION FOR SPEAKING
OPENING STATEMENTS

> **Language note**
>
> In law, an opening statement is made by each side at the start of a trial. During their opening statements, which are usually quite brief, the two sides in a case outline their version of the facts to the judge and/or jury. In a debate, the opening statement serves a similar purpose. Each side presents their main argument to the audience before going into greater detail during the debate. In a trial, the judge or jury decide on a party's guilt (in criminal law) or liability (in civil law). In a debate, the audience decide on the winning side by voting for the debating team that had the best arguments.

1 🔊 1.5 👤 Ask the class to guess what an opening statement is. Elicit an explanation of the term 'opening statement' from the class (see Language note above). Tell the students to quickly read the four questions so that they know what to listen out for. Play the recording and ask the students to answer the questions. At the end of the recording, ask the students to check their answers with a partner. Elicit the answers from the class.

> **Answers**
>
> 1 Keeping animals in zoos helps to protect them; it educates people about animals. We should support zoos.
> 2 Zoos protect animals; they educate our children; modern zoos are comfortable and in good condition.
> 3 Many endangered species (e.g. the giant panda, the snow leopard) are kept safe in zoos; speaker learnt about exotic animals as a child after being taken to the zoo; animals in zoos now have large areas which resemble their natural habitat.
> 4 A summary and a recommendation to visit zoos or give financial support.

2 🔊 1.5 👤 Ask the students to read the notes in the box to find out how 'signposting language' is used during public speaking. Then ask the students to read the 12 examples of signposting language. Play the recording again and ask the class to circle the examples of signposting language that they hear. Quickly go through the answers with the class.

> **Answers**
> 2, 7, 10, 12

3 👥 Give the students two minutes to complete the task in pairs. Elicit the answers from the class.

> **Answers**
> 1 1, 2   2 3, 6, 7   3 8, 10

> **Language note**
>
> Learners of English often stress syllables that would usually be unstressed. This is especially true of words that contain the schwa sound, which is the unstressed vowel sound (as in moth*er*), written as the /ə/ symbol in the International Phonetic Alphabet (IPA). When grammar words such as of, some, a, the and to are said together with other words, the vowel sound in each becomes weak. Compare the stressed forms of to and the with their unstressed forms when used as part of a sentence:
>
> to /tuː/   the /ðiː/
> to the shops /təðə'ʃɒps/
>
> When used in normal everyday speech, there are no artificial pauses between the words. They run together, and the vowels in the grammar words that link them become weak.

PRONUNCIATION FOR SPEAKING

4 👤 🔊 1.6 Do the first extract together as a class. Point out that the words in the signposting phrases run together. The phrases are pronounced as one speech unit, or 'chunk'. It is important that your students hear and understand this, as many learners of English overstress individual words, which can be distracting and lead to misunderstandings. Play the rest of the recording and ask the students to underline the stressed syllable in each signposting expression.

> **Answers**
> 2 For ex<u>a</u>mple
> 3 An<u>o</u>ther point is that
> 4 To <u>su</u>mmarize the main points
> 5 <u>Fi</u>nally

5 🔊 1.6 Play the first extract again and then repeat the phrase First of all. Signal to the class that they should repeat it. Repeat the phrase, again asking the class to repeat it back. Continue until you are satisfied that most people are pronouncing it correctly. Repeat this procedure for each of the extracts.

6 👥 Ask the students to read the information box on introducing examples. Then ask them to complete the arguments with their own examples.

7 👥 Ask the students to read the information box on expressing general beliefs. With a higher-level class, you could point out that it makes your argument even stronger if you can attribute the claim being made to a particular source (e.g. It's believed that animals suffer from being kept in cages. A recent article in Psychology Today suggested that animals in zoos are less happy than those in the wild).

Ask the students to think of a topic that interests them and about which they have an opinion. For example, sport, fashion, computers or books. Then ask them to work in pairs and complete the three sentences with their own ideas about their chosen topic. Ask the students to write the sentences down. Monitor the pairs as they work, giving feedback as appropriate. Give the students 2–3 minutes to complete the sentences, then elicit ideas from the class, giving feedback on the language used. You could encourage discussion by inviting students to comment on the statements made.

SPEAKING TASK
PREPARE

1 👤 Remind the class of the debate topic: Using animals for entertainment should be banned. Ask them to decide if they are for or against using animals for entertainment, and give them five minutes to take notes to support their opinion.

2 👤 Give the students five minutes to develop their three strongest arguments. If they have access to the internet, you could give them 10–15 minutes to research the topic online.

3 👤 Give the students 5–10 minutes to sketch out their final notes according to the outline in the box. Encourage them to write their ideas in note form so that when they refer to them during their talk they will sound more fluent. You could point out that it is often very dull to listen to someone reading prepared sentences out loud. Using notes encourages a more natural delivery, although may require more preparation and confidence.

PRACTISE

4 👥 Students complete the task in pairs, each reading their statement out once. Remind the students that their statements should be about two minutes long. Tell students to time each other and to say when two minutes have passed, at which point the student speaking must finish off his or her statement. Allow up to five minutes for the complete task.

5 👥 Give the students five minutes to give each other feedback and up to five minutes to make any changes to their outline notes based on the feedback they are given.

PRESENT

6 👥 Students present their opening statements in groups of three. You could try to make sure that both sides of the debate are represented in each group by getting a show of hands for or against the statement and organizing the groups accordingly. Allow up to 10 minutes for the delivery of the opening statements and encourage follow-up discussion.

Optional activity

You could ask each group to decide which member of their group gave the best opening statement. Those students then give their opening statements to the whole class. Once each student has given their opening statements, the class then vote (either on paper or by a show of hands) for the person they think gave the best statement. This can be beneficial in several ways. It can give the student elected to speak in front of the class a huge confidence boost, whether or not they win the final vote; it shows the other students that speaking in front of a class in English is possible, and may encourage the quieter students to be more forthcoming; finally, it gives all members of the group the chance to participate in three aspects of a genuine debate, giving the opening statements, listening to and following arguments presented, and voting on the best speaker.

TASK CHECKLIST AND OBJECTIVES REVIEW

Refer students to the end of each unit for the Task checklist and Objectives review. Students complete the tables individually to reflect on their learning and identify areas for improvement.

WORDLIST

See Teaching tips, pages 9–11 for ideas about how to make the most of the Wordlist with your students.

REVIEW TEST

See pages 98–99 for the photocopiable Review test for this unit, and page 91 for ideas about when and how to administer the Review test.

ADDITIONAL SPEAKING TASK

See page 118 for an Additional speaking task related to this unit.

Put students in groups of four and focus them on the job advert. Then, ask them to read their role (A, B, C or D). Point out that students A and B are interviewers who work for the zoo. Students C and D would like the job. Put students A and C together, and students B and D together, to conduct the interviewers. After five minutes, swap pairs so that A and D are working together, and B and C are working together. They repeat the interviews. Then, ask students A and B who they would choose to fill the job position.

RESEARCH PROJECT

Give a lecture on the most endangered species in the world.

Divide the class into groups and ask each group to investigate the most endangered species. Students can search for 'the top-ten endangered species in the world'. Give each group one of the animals listed and ask them to find out about their behaviour, diet, their natural environment and other interesting facts. Students could use tools on the Cambridge LMS, for example the wiki, to share their initial research with the rest the class.

Each group will then prepare a 15-minute presentation, including time for questions. Learners could develop the wiki further with their final research and refer to this during their presentation, create slides using presentation software and produce a leaflet to email to the rest of the class.

2 CUSTOMS AND TRADITIONS

Learning objectives

Before you start the *Unlock your knowledge* section, ask students to read the Learning objectives box. This will give them a clear idea of what they will learn in the unit. Tell them that you will return to these objectives at the end of the unit, when they review what they have learned. Give students the opportunity to ask any questions they might have.

UNLOCK YOUR KNOWLEDGE

Background information

The photo shows people selling fresh flowers, fruit and vegetables at one of Bangkok's floating markets. Bangkok, the capital of Thailand, has many canals, and only recently have these been renovated and cleaned, allowing these traditional marketplaces to open and begin trading again.

👥 Allow 4–5 minutes for students to discuss the questions in pairs and then invite feedback from the class. Select one pair and ask them for a summary of their responses.

WATCH AND LISTEN

▶ Video script

Japan is an island nation made up of a group of islands surrounded by the sea. The island of Japan has a population of just under 130 million people. This population is falling as people age, and fewer and fewer babies are born.

In Japan, the average life expectancy is 79 for Japanese men, and Japanese women live even longer with an average age of 86.

On the main island of Honshu is a small town called Toba. Here, a 2,000-year-old tradition is being kept alive by a group of women who are in their 80s. They are *ama* divers. *Ama* means a sea person.

Ama are normally women. This is because the Japanese believe that women have more fat in their bodies which helps keep them warm in the cold water. Diving keeps them fit and feeling young.

Many of this generation have been diving since they left school in their teens. The women free dive without tanks of oxygen, but they wear white clothing which is meant to protect the women from shark attacks. The *ama* believe sharks don't like the colour white.

ama divers used to dive for pearls, but due to large pearl farms this practice is now no longer profitable. *Ama* now dive mainly for seafood. The women cook their freshest fish straight from the sea.

Meanwhile, all over Japan, people are celebrating the arrival of spring and the cherry blossom, or *sakura*. Cherry blossom is a national symbol of Japan. The flowers are white or pink.

During the spring, there are programmes every day on TV that tell people when the flowers will arrive. When they arrive, everyone in the towns, cities and countryside joins in the celebrations. People go to parks and gardens to look at the flowers. They take lots of photos on their phones and cameras. People eat and drink under the trees, and celebrations carry on well into the night.

PREPARING TO WATCH

UNDERSTANDING KEY VOCABULARY

1 👤👥 Give the students 3–5 minutes to read the sentences and match the words with the definitions, either individually or with a partner.

Answers

a alive
b generation
c pearl
d identity
e dive(d)
f life expectancy
g blossom
h die out

PREDICTING FROM VISUALS

2 👥 Students work together in small groups. Ask them to do task 1 as a guessing task, each taking it in turn to describe a photograph while the other students guess which is being described.

3 ▶ Play the video for students to check their ideas.

Answers

The first two photographs show the *ama* pearl divers of Japan. The last two photographs show the Cherry Blossom festival, also in Japan.

WHILE WATCHING

UNDERSTANDING MAIN IDEAS

4 ▶ 👥 Ask the students to read the questions and to try and guess the answers with a partner before watching the video. Then play the video again for students to check.

> **Answers**
> 1, 2, 4, 5, 6, 8

UNDERSTANDING DETAIL

5 👤👥 Students complete the task individually and check their answers in pairs. Do not give feedback at this point.

6 ▶ Play the video again for students to check.

> **Answers**
> 1 F 2 T 3 T 4 F 5 T 6 F 7 F 8 F

DISCUSSION

7 👥 Put students into groups for this discussion. Allow about three minutes for this, before inviting feedback from the class.

LISTENING 1

PREPARING TO LISTEN

UNDERSTANDING KEY VOCABULARY

1 👤 Allow 2–3 minutes for students to complete the task individually and then check their answers in pairs. Quickly go through the answers with the class.

> **Answers**
> 1 many different cultures
> 2 no longer exists
> 3 do things together
> 4 get used
> 5 made for the first time
> 6 cause it to change
> 7 human culture and society
> 8 an important date in the past

PREDICTING CONTENT

2 ◀) 2.1 👤 Students complete the task individually. Go through the answers with the class. Ask them what an *anthropologist* is

(someone who scientifically studies humans and their customs, beliefs and relationships). They should be able to guess this from the word *anthropology* in the previous task and from the advert.

> **Answers**
> 1 an anthropologist
> 2 traditions in the modern world
> 3 Sunday, 1300 GMT

WHILE LISTENING

LISTENING FOR MAIN IDEAS

3 ◀) 2.2 👤 Students complete the task individually and then check their answers in pairs. Quickly go through the answers with the class.

> **Answers**
> A shaking hands
> (the other pictures show: B playing board games, C listening to the radio, D watching television, E sending greetings cards, F preparing food)

LISTENING FOR DETAIL

4 ◀) 2.2 👤 Ask the students to answer the questions from what they can remember of the recording. Then play the recording a second time and ask the students to check their answers.

> **Answers**
> 1 b 2 b 3 b 4 a 5 b 6 b

PRONUNCIATION FOR LISTENING

> **Language note**
>
> We usually pronounce a /t/ or /d/ sound if it is in the final position in a word, and if it is followed by a vowel sound. However, we don't always pronounce /t/ or /d/ if it is followed by a consonant sound.

5 ◀) 2.3 👤 Ask the students to underline the final /t/ and /d/ sounds that they think that they will be able to hear in each sentence. Then play the recording and ask the students to check their answers. Ask the students to briefly discuss any differences between their original guesses and what they actually heard. Then play the recording again to give the students a second opportunity to listen carefully to the sounds. Elicit from the class the final /t/ and /d/ sounds that were heard clearly and go through the answers together. If the class found it difficult to distinguish the sounds, play the recording a third time.

Answers

Students should be able to hear the yellow highlighted sounds clearly. These are /t/ or /d/ sounds followed by a vowel sound. The green highlighted /t/ and /d/ sounds are less easy to hear.

6 ◀) 2.4 👥👥👥 Ask students to practise saying the sentences in small groups. They should repeat the sentences a few times each.

POST-LISTENING

Language note

During a talk, a speaker can talk about **causes**. To introduce causes, a speaker can use phrases like: *Due to ...*, *The reason for this is ...*, *because ...*, etc. In addition, the speaker can also introduce **effects**, using phrases like *That's why ...*, *This means ...*, etc. Understanding phrases to talk about cause and effect can help students organize notes during a lecture.

7 ◀) 2.5 👤 Students complete the task individually. With a stronger class, you could ask the students to complete the gaps using the words presented in the language box before playing the recording.

Answers

1 That's why
2 because
3 due to
4 The reason for this is
5 This means

8 👥 Do the first question with the class to make sure they understand what they have to do. Then ask the students to work in pairs and answer questions 1–5.

Answers

1 <u>As a child, I lived in Japan, Thailand and Egypt</u>. That's why ⟨I decided to study Anthropology.⟩
2 ⟨Some traditions die out⟩because <u>our way of life changes</u>.

3 <u>Now, due to developments in technology, ⟨people spend more time playing games on their phones.⟩</u>
4 ⟨But now we don't have to work so hard.⟩ The reason for this is <u>we have modern kitchens and supermarket food</u>.
5 <u>You can find any recipe you want on the internet.</u> This means that ⟨many people don't need recipe books any more.⟩

9 👤 Students complete the task individually and then check their answers in pairs. Quickly go through the answers with the class.

Answers

1 Because
2 That's why
3 This means that
4 because
5 Because of

DISCUSSION

10 👥👥👥 Elicit some national traditions from the class and ask the students which of these are still important for their country. Encourage class discussion for 1–2 minutes, then ask the students to discuss the questions in small groups. Allow five minutes, then ask the first group to report back to the class. Ask the second group if they discussed anything that hasn't already been said, and continue around the groups. Ask questions to encourage class discussion. If a group makes a potentially contentious statement, ask the class if they agree with what has been said, and why.

⊙ LANGUAGE DEVELOPMENT

SUFFIXES

1 👤 Students complete the task individually and then check their answers in pairs. Quickly go through the answers with the class. Challenge the class to complete the task in under a minute.

Answers

2 verb 3 adjective 4 verb 5 noun 6 noun
7 noun 8 verb

2 Students complete the task individually and then check their answers in pairs. Quickly go through the answers with the class.

> **Answers**
>
> 1 celebration 2 acceptable 3 equipment
> 4 political 5 shorten 6 specialise/specialize

> **Language note**
>
> Words such as *specialize* can be spelled with both *-ise* and *-ize* in British English (*specialise*; *specialize*). In American English, usually the *-ize* ending is used. You could point out to the class that although both are used in British English, it is important to be consistent (i.e. try not to use both *-ise* and *-ize* endings in the same text).

3 Students read the notes on suffixes with meaning and complete the task individually. Elicit the answers from the class. Make sure that the students are clear on the rules a–c about suffixes.

> **Answers**
>
> a -ful b -less c -able

> **Language note**
>
> The suffixes *-able* and *-ible* both mean 'can be', or 'suitable for'. If we don't change the root word, then we use *-able*. But if we change the root word, (e.g. *eat → edible*) then we use *-ible*.
> The suffix *-able/ible* can be affixed to several verbs to form a new word.

4 Students complete the task individually and then check their answers in pairs. Quickly go through the answers with the class. Point out that if we want to add the *-able/ible* suffix to a verb ending in *-y*, then we need to change the *-y* to an *i*.

> **Answers**
>
> 1 harmless 2 useful; reliable; careful 3 enjoyable
> 4 thoughtless

5 Give the students 2–3 minutes to discuss the task in pairs or small groups, then elicit ideas from the class. Encourage discussion where there is disagreement, asking the students to support their ideas with examples.

DEPENDENT PREPOSITIONS

6 Students read the information box on dependent prepositions and complete the task individually. Elicit the answers from the class.

> **Answers**
>
> 2 with 3 in 4 to 5 about 6 for

7 Students complete the task individually and then check their answers in pairs. Quickly go through the answers with the class. You could point out to students that *listen for* (more commonly: *listen out for*) is correct in some contexts. If you listen (out) for something, then you are making an effort to hear a noise that you are expecting. For example, *Would you listen out for the phone while I'm in the garden.*

> **Answers**
>
> 2 to   3 for   4 from   5 of; on

8 Students complete the task in pairs. You could also do this as a group activity. Tell the students to begin with the question(s) that they find the most interesting. Allow 3–5 minutes for discussion. Invite the students to share any particularly interesting points or observations that came up during their discussions. Encourage class discussion where possible.

LISTENING 2

PREPARING TO LISTEN

UNDERSTANDING KEY VOCABULARY

1 Students complete the task individually and then check their answers in pairs. Quickly go through the answers with the class. As a follow-up task, you could ask the students in pairs or groups to discuss any of the sentences that apply to them, or which reflect something similar to their own lives. For example, were any of the students badly behaved as children? Do they use social-networking sites to keep in touch with friends? Or, more interestingly, do any of them *not* use social-networking sites?

> **Answers**
>
> 1 c 2 e 3 a 4 f 5 b 6 d 7 h 8 g

USING YOUR KNOWLEDGE

2 Elicit ideas from the class, but do not feed back yet on whether their suggestions are correct or not. Try to get at least three ideas concerning modern ways of behaving. Other suggestions might include the use of smartphones (for texting, playing games or using other apps), downloading music rather than buying physical media and a greater tendency to find work away from the place in which a person grew up.

3 ◀) 2.6 👤 Students complete the task individually. Quickly elicit the answers from the class.

4 👥 Students complete the task in small groups. Ask each group to appoint a secretary to summarize the discussion for the class at the end of the task. Allow up to five minutes for discussion. Elicit a summary of the discussion from the first group, then invite the other groups to add any further points not already covered.

> ### Optional activity
>
> Write the following on the board: *Facebook, LinkedIn.* Ask the class what the two have in common (they are both social-networking sites) and what is different between them (LinkedIn is more commonly used as a professional network, whereas Facebook is used for both personal and professional social networking). Elicit other social networks from the class (suggestions may include, among others, Xing (professional networking), Bebo (general, popular with children), Myspace (general, popular with musicians, lost a lot of users to Facebook), Twitter (general, micro-blogging) and Flickr (mainly used for sharing photos). Find out whether there are any social networks that are particular to their region, or especially popular with people from their country. Ask the class to outline the main uses of the different social networks and find out who uses which social network(s), and for what.

WHILE LISTENING

LISTENING FOR MAIN IDEAS

5 ◀) 2.7 👤 Students complete the task individually. Quickly elicit the answers from the class.

> ### Answers
>
> Social networking and behaviour on social networks, such as sharing photos; posting 'happy birthday' on people's walls; using the 'like' button.

6 ◀) 2.7 👥 Elicit the answer to the first question from the class. Students then complete the task in pairs. Quickly elicit the answers from the class.

> ### Answers
>
> 1 because it's too easy to do
> 2 because the friend didn't enjoy the actual experience
> 3 posting photos/videos online is fine, it's acceptable
> 4 people want to boast – they want to appear to be having a good life
> 5 the speaker is against sharing information online
> 6 the speaker is talking about the benefits, when you live far from family

POST-LISTENING

> ### Language note
>
> We can use signposting phrases (*in my opinion, I think that …, I believe that …*, etc.) so that the listener knows we are going to give an opinion.
>
> We can use phrases like *I could not agree more*, or *I'm not convinced* to make it clear that we agree or disagree with something.

7 ◀) 2.8 👥 Students complete the task in pairs. With a stronger group, you could ask the students to try and complete the phrases from memory, and then listen to the recording to check their work and complete any unfinished phrases. Go through the answers with the class. Note that in informal situations, *I **could not** agree more* would often be contracted to *I **couldn't** agree more*.

> ### Answers
>
> 2 pointless 3 agree 4 disagree 5 convinced
> 6 Personally 7 agree

8 👤 Students complete the task individually and check their answers in pairs. Quickly elicit the answers from the class.

> ### Answers
>
> | signposting an opinion | agreeing | disagreeing |
> |---|---|---|
> | It seems … to me. What about …? Why not …? Personally, I …. I think that … | I couldn't agree more. I totally agree. | It seems pointless to me. I completely disagree. I'm not convinced. I don't agree. |

DISCUSSION

9 Give the students up to five minutes to discuss the task in small groups, then elicit ideas from the class. Encourage the students to support their ideas with examples from their own experiences of social networking. Quickly elicit one or two ideas from each group. If the group seems keen to discuss their ideas further, allow a few more minutes for class discussion. Try to keep the discussion lively by limiting the time each student has to speak and respond to the points made. If possible, try to elicit ideas for discussion from the quieter students. Avoid agreeing and disagreeing with the students. Instead, encourage the students to support their ideas and question each other's ideas where there is disagreement in the group.

CRITICAL THINKING

UNDERSTAND

1 Ask the class to look at the ideas map and to identify its main topic.

Answer

social-networking activities

2 Elicit one extra idea from the class. Ideas could include, among others, posting news stories, advertising jobs, inviting people to parties, publicizing events or getting in touch with old friends with whom you have lost contact. Give the students 2–3 minutes to complete the task in pairs.

3 Give the students up to five minutes to complete the task in small groups.

APPLY

4 Ask the two pairs in each group to swap partners so that each student is working with a new partner. One student in each pair should prepare an ideas map on 'new ways of communicating' and the other should prepare an ideas map on 'traditional ways of communicating'. Give the students 2–3 minutes to prepare their ideas maps. Then ask them to go through their ideas maps with their partners, making changes according to their partners' ideas.

5 Ask students to team up with a new pair of students and give the groups up to five minutes to complete the task. Monitor the groups as they discuss their work. If you have time, you could invite one group to draw their ideas map on the board and use it as the basis of a class discussion.

ANALYZE

6 Quickly elicit the answers from the class.

Answers

1 D 2 A 3 A 4 A 5 D 6 D

EVALUATE

7 Give the students 5–10 minutes to discuss the questions in small groups. Encourage them to use examples from their own experience and to use the language used when discussing advantages and disadvantages. Monitor the groups giving feedback during or at the end of the task as appropriate. When the discussions seem to be quieting down, give the students a few moments to finish what they have to say, then quickly elicit 2–3 ideas from each group. If there is time, invite the class to comment on the points each group makes.

SPEAKING

PREPARATION FOR SPEAKING

1 Ask the class to read the information box. If necessary, explain *interrupt* (to stop someone speaking because you want to say something). You could invite the students to give you some suggestions as to how we can interrupt politely. Give feedback as appropriate, but avoid too much comment as examples will be given in Exercise 1. Then ask the students to complete the task individually and check their answers in pairs.

Answers

1 I'm sorry to interrupt
2 You may be right but
3 Yes I understand but
4 But what about
5 I see your point
6 I disagree

2 👤 Students complete the task individually and check their answers in pairs. Quickly elicit the answers from the class. You could add further suggestions from the group.

> **Answers**
>
> b what about
> c I disagree; I completely disagree
> d I see your point; (yes) I understand, but; you may be right, but

3 👥 Give the students their roles, and ask them to read the instructions individually. You could check that the students have understood their roles by asking Student As: *Do you think social networking is good or bad?* (good) Student Bs: *Do you think social networking is good or bad?* (bad). Then give the students 3–5 minutes to complete the task in pairs. Remind them that they should stick to their roles, whether or not they agree with them. You could give them a few moments at the end of the task to give their real opinions, to say how much they agree with the opinions they expressed during the task. Quickly elicit the key arguments made by Students A and B around the class.

4 👤 Ask the students to read the explanation box and to find out how they can make their points more strongly when discussing their ideas. You could write *I agree* on the board and ask the class how to make the phrase on the board sound stronger by eliciting 'I strongly agree' or 'I totally agree'. Note that 'I really agree' is much less common, but not incorrect. Ask the students to complete the task, quickly elicit the answers from the class when they are finished.

> **Answers**
>
> | signposting an opinion | agreeing | disagreeing |
> |---|---|---|
> | I (strongly) believe that … I'm (absolutely) convinced that … I (really) think that … | I (totally) agree. Yes, that's (completely) true. That's (definitely) right. It's (absolutely) true. | I'm (really) not convinced. I (completely) disagree. It's (absolutely) not true. I'm (totally) against … |

PRONUNICATION FOR SPEAKING

5 🔊 2.9 👤 Students complete the task individually and check their answers in pairs. Quickly elicit the answers from the class. If several students are having difficulty hearing the stressed words, play the recording again.

> **Answers**
>
> 1b completely
> 2b really
> 3b strongly
> 4b absolutely

6 👥 Students complete the task in pairs, taking it in turns to say the sentences out loud and giving each other feedback. Monitor the pairs, making sure that they correctly stress the adverbs. Try to listen to each student speak at least once if possible.

7 👤 Students complete the task individually. Elicit two or three suggestions from the class once they are ready, then go on to Exercise 8.

8 👥 👥👥 Give the students 3–5 minutes to discuss their ideas in pairs or small groups. Finish off by eliciting some more ideas from the students. Invite the class to comment on any particularly interesting opinions.

9 👤 Ask the class to read the explanation box. You could elicit complete sentences from two or three students to help set up the next activity. If so, let the students know whether their suggested sentences are correct or incorrect, but avoid giving too much feedback at this stage as the students will be given another opportunity to make their own sentences in Exercise 10. Once the language point and task are clear, students should complete the task individually and check their answers in pairs. Quickly elicit the answers from the class.

> **Answers**
>
> a 1, 3, 5, 7
> b 2, 4, 6, 8

10 👤 Students complete the task individually. Set a strict time limit of three minutes (two for a stronger class) to encourage students to complete the task quickly.

11 👥 👥👥 Give the students up to five minutes to discuss their ideas in pairs or small groups. Tell them that they do not need to go through all of their completed phrases. They should focus on the ideas that interest them the most. Finish off by eliciting some of the ideas discussed from the students. Invite the class to comment on any particularly interesting or surprising opinions.

Language note

Although it is possible to start a sentence with *I disagree that*, the phrase *I disagree with* is much more common. The following sentences each express similar ideas, but in a slightly different way.

- *I **disagree with** using social networks.* (= Social networks should not be used.)
- *I **disagree that** using social networks is a good idea.* (= Using social networks is a bad idea.)
- *I **disagree with** the notion that using social networks is a good idea.* (= Using social networks is a bad idea. / The idea that using social networks is a good idea is wrong.)

Note that the following sentence is not possible *I disagree **that** using social networks.*

SPEAKING TASK

Optional activity

If you are teaching a relatively young group, it may be that the modern technology referred to during this unit will not appear especially modern to your students, who will probably have grown up with email, Skype, smart phones, social networking and the internet. To make this task more interesting to them, the students could ask the discussion question to a parent, grandparent or older relative or friend as a homework task in preparation for the discussion. Ideally, they would interview someone who grew up before the invention of the internet and mobile/smartphones, but who has since had experience of communicating using new technologies. At the start of the next lesson, the students could then get together in pairs and compare notes from their interviews, using these as a basis for their ideas maps.

PREPARE

1 👥 Give the students up to five minutes to draft their ideas maps in pairs. If you set the optional homework task above, ask the students to use the notes they took during their interviews as the basis for their ideas maps.

2 👥 Set a strict time limit of two minutes for this task. Then, elicit examples of positive and negative aspects from the class. You could put these in a table on the board. For example:

positive aspects	negative aspects
We are always able to contact friends and colleagues.	*We are often disturbed by calls, texts or emails.*
We can do much more with our phones than simply make phone calls.	*Phones go out of date very quickly, and it can be expensive to upgrade.*

Quickly elicit as many ideas for each side as possible. You could keep things lively by going round the class and asking students for positive and negative aspects in turn. Complete the table as the students give you their ideas. Some students may disagree as to whether something is positive or negative, but avoid commenting at this stage – simply complete the table with the students' suggestions.

As a follow-up class discussion, you could ask the class whether they all agree with the ideas expressed. Try to elicit the idea that what is a positive aspect for some people could be negative for others, or that some aspects could be both positive and negative, depending on the circumstances. An obvious example would be that smartphone ownership means that many of us are now constantly available, and always able to check and respond to emails, phone calls, text messages and social-networking notifications, etc.

PRACTISE

3 👥👥 Give the students 5–10 minutes to discuss their opinions in small groups. Remind them to use the language presented earlier in the unit on agreeing and disagreeing. Monitor the groups as they discuss their ideas maps, giving feedback as appropriate and taking notes to use as the basis of a class feedback session at the end of the task. You could try to draw the discussions to a conclusion when they seem to be coming to an end by asking each group to take a vote on whether the effects of modern technology have been largely negative or largely positive. This could then lead to a wider class debate, but beware of asking the students to repeat too many of the arguments that they may already have expressed several times by now. If possible, pick up on one or two especially interesting points that you heard as you monitored the group discussions and encourage the class to debate these ideas in more depth.

4 👥 Give the students 3–5 minutes to discuss the questions in small groups. When the groups have finished, ask them to consider how they might improve their performance next time. Give them up to two minutes to discuss this second question in their groups, and tell them to be ready to offer some practical suggestions to the rest of the class.

DISCUSS

5 👥 Put students in different groups to repeat the discussion task.

TASK CHECKLIST AND OBJECTIVES REVIEW

Refer students to the end of each unit for the Task checklist and Objectives review. Students complete the tables individually to reflect on their learning and identify areas for improvement.

WORDLIST

See Teaching tips, pages 9–11 for ideas about how to make the most of the Wordlist with your students.

REVIEW TEST

See pages 100–101 for the photocopiable Review test for this unit, and page 91 for ideas about when and how to administer the Review test.

ADDITIONAL SPEAKING TASK

See page 119 for an Additional speaking task related to this unit.

Put students in small groups of three or four. Give them the questions and allow a minute for them to make notes. Students then discuss the ideas. Allow five or six minutes for the interaction and monitor to make sure students are taking turns equally. Students then report back on their group's discussion to the rest of the class.

RESEARCH PROJECT

Discuss customs and traditions with learners in another country.

Ask the class to think about their own customs and traditions. You could ask them to think about special foods, culture, time of year and why they are important. Students can use the tools on the Cambridge CLMS to share their ideas with each other.

Tell the class they will be contacting students in other countries to find out about customs and traditions in those countries. You can search for 'international school collaboration' in advance to explore the options for doing this. Students can send audio/video messages to other students or set up online live video sessions to discuss customs and traditions.

3 HISTORY

UNLOCK YOUR KNOWLEDGE

Background note

The photograph shows the ruins of Machu Picchu, a 15th-century Inca site in Peru. This 'lost city' is located 2,430 metres above sea level and was originally built in around 1450. It was abandoned a hundred years later, and only discovered in 1911. It is now one of the most famous tourist sites in the world, and a symbol of the great Inca civilization.

👥 Ask students to discuss questions 1–4 in pairs. Give the students two minutes, then quickly elicit one place that from each student that they would like to visit. Find out which historical places the students suggested from their own country. Write the suggestions from their own country on the board, then finish off by asking the students to rank the places in order of interest to foreign tourists.

WATCH AND LISTEN

▶ Video script

In the dry Atacama Desert in Peru, the sands reveal treasures more valuable than gold: the objects and remains of an ancient Peruvian people called the Chiribaya.

Hundreds of years ago, the dry air and sand of the desert naturally preserved and mummified the dead bodies of the Chiribaya people. For archaeologists, these mummies are silent and powerful witnesses of ancient history.

The Chiribaya people lived in southern Peru, in a valley from the Pacific coast to around 40 kilometres inland. At one time, there were 30,000 people living in the valley, but not much is known about the culture of the Chiribaya people. Their simple buildings made of mud and sticks did not survive.

Everything archaeologists know about the Chiribaya comes from their tombs. They have discovered many treasures buried with the mummies, such as gold cups, earrings and decorations.

However the archaeology has brought thieves looking for gold.

"Greedy, greedy people. Just tomb after tomb. They would just get the mummy bundles or get the mummies and the word was that the gold was inside the mouth so they would separate the skull from the rest of the body and crack the skull. It's just awful and annoying that we can't stop it."

Archaeologists must work fast to beat the thieves. A new tomb has been discovered. Inside the tomb is a complete mummy, wrapped in a striped blanket, with an offering of llama feet in a basket to represent food.

In a laboratory, the archaeologists unwrap the body. The head has grey hair. They then remove the body's blankets. This mummy was a very old man. The way his body was preserved shows he was an important member of Chiribaya society.

It is the job of archaeologists to help reveal the secrets of the Chiribaya people. However, because of the destruction of the mummies by treasure hunters, many mysteries of these ancient people will never be solved.

PREPARING TO WATCH

UNDERSTANDING KEY VOCABULARY

1 👤 Students complete the task individually and check their answers in pairs.

> **Answers**
> 1 c 2 a 3 e 4 b 5 f 6 d

Optional activity

👤👥 Challenge the students to be the first, either individually or in pairs, to write a grammatically correct sentence or short paragraph using all six words from Exercise 1. As soon as the first student is ready, they should raise their hand and give you the sentence. If it is correct, the student has 'won'. If not, tell the other students to carry on writing their sentences and tell the student with the incorrect sentence to correct it for you to look at later. Continue like this until you have a correct sentence. Finish by correcting the incorrect sentences as a class. Give the student who wrote the sentence being corrected the first chance to correct it. With a weaker class, you may prefer to do this optional task following Exercise 7.

PREDICTING CONTENT FROM VISUALS

2 👥 Give the students up to two minutes to discuss the task in pairs, then elicit ideas from the class. Encourage the students to support their ideas with evidence from the photographs.

3 ▶ 👤 Students complete the task individually and check their answers in pairs. Quickly elicit the answers from the class.

> **Answers**
>
> The person in the photograph is an archaelogist; she is working in the Atacama desert, examining a mummy.

WHILE WATCHING

UNDERSTANDING MAIN IDEAS

4 ▶ 👤👥 Students complete the task individually and compare their answers in pairs. Students watch the video again to check their answers.

> **Answers**
>
> 1 archaeologists 2 tombs 3 buried 4 treasures
> 5 discover 6 laboratory 7 preserved

5 👤 Students complete the task individually and compare their answers in pairs. Elicit the ideas from the class; with a stronger class, you could also ask them to try and remember what information is given about each of the topics mentioned in the video.

> **Answers**
>
> 2, 4, 5, 6

UNDERSTANDING DETAIL

6 ▶ 👤 Students complete the task individually. Quickly go through the answers with the class. With a stronger group, you could ask the students to rewrite the false sentences to make them correct (or to correct them orally).

> **Answers**
>
> 1 T 2 F 3 F 4 T 5 T

DISCUSSION

7 👥 Give the students 2–3 minutes to complete the table together. Put a copy of the table on the board and open this task up as a class discussion. Encourage the students to support their ideas with examples by asking questions such as *Why do archaeologists have to be fit? Why might they need a good sense of humour? Why is creativity important for archeologists?*

As a follow up, you could ask the students if they know of any archaeologists from books or films, and how realistic the portrayal of fictional archaeologists is. Probably the most well known fictional archeologist is Indiana Jones, originally portrayed in the movie *Raiders of the Lost Ark* (1981). More recently, films such as *The Mummy* and *Tomb Raider* have also featured archaeologists as action heroes.

8 👥 This question follows on naturally from the class discussion in Exercise 7, so finish off this section by asking the class for a show of hands: *Who would like to be an archeologist? Who wouldn't?* Then elicit reasons from the class.

LISTENING 1

PREPARING TO LISTEN

UNDERSTANDING KEY VOCABULARY

1 👤 Students complete the task individually and compare their answers in pairs. Quickly go through the answers with the class.

> **Answers**
>
> 1 g 2 j 3 d 4 c 5 a 6 e 7 h 8 f 9 b 10 i

USING YOUR KNOWLEDGE

2 👥 Students complete the task in small groups. Give them up to three minutes to tell each other what they know about the historical finds, then go through the answers with the class and try to elicit some information about each of the finds.

> **Answers**
>
> 1 D 2 A 3 E 4 B 5 C

WHILE LISTENING

LISTENING FOR MAIN IDEAS

3 ◄) 3.1 👤 Students complete the task individually. Quickly elicit the historical finds discussed.

> **Answers**
> They discuss the Terracotta Army, the Rosetta Stone, and Tutankhamen's tomb.

PRONUNCIATION FOR LISTENING

> **Optional activity**
>
> Before doing Exercise 4, ask the students to read the information box on connected speech. If you feel comfortable occasionally using the students' first language during the class, you could demonstrate weak forms by giving them a sentence in their language and asking them to say it quickly and naturally, as if it were part of a conversation. Encourage the students to notice that not all words are pronounced as clearly in sentences as they would be when said out loud as individual words. This might help focus weaker students on what they need to listen out for in Exercise 4.

4 ◄) 3.2 👤 Students complete the task individually. As a follow up, you could ask them to write the /ə/ sound above the vowels where it can be heard in the highlighted words. You could also ask them to say the words individually, and notice the difference in pronunciation between when they are said as part of a sentence and when they are said individually.

5 ◄) 3.3 👥 👥👥 Give students 2–3 minutes to practise the pronunciation in pairs or small groups. Then go through each sentence with the whole group. Begin by modeling sentence 1, then gesture to the class to get them to repeat what you said. Repeat the first sentence a few times, then quickly elicit the sentence from individual students. If a student does not pronounce the weak forms correctly, get them to repeat the sentence again. If the student still gets it wrong, get the whole class to model the sentence again. Repeat in this manner until the student says the sentence correctly, then go on to the other sentences and repeat the procedure.

6 ◄) 3.1 👤 Students complete the task individually and check their answers in pairs. Quickly go through the answers with the class.

> **Answers**
>
> | Who was the ruler? | King Ptolomy V | Emperor Qin Shi Huang | King Tutankhamun |
> | --- | --- | --- | --- |
> | How many years old is the historical find? | More than 2,000 years old | More than 2,000 years old | About 3,500 years old |
> | When was it discovered? | 1799 | the 1940s | 1922 |
> | What did we learn from this? | Learned about hieroglyphics, about ancient Egyptian beliefs and culture | How the Chinese army was organized and what weapons they used | About life in ancient Egypt and their religious beliefs |

POST-LISTENING

7 ◄) 3.4 👤 Students listen to the recording and focus on the expressions used to show that a person is paying attention.

8 👤 👥👥 Students complete the task individually or in pairs. As a follow-up task, you could ask the students to role-play the dialogues in pairs. The most likely answers are below. However, depending on the intonation, some of the phrases could have other functions as well. For example, 'uhuh' could also be used to show understanding, and possibly even to show agreement.

> **Answers**
>
> 1 I think so; Yes you're right; That's a good idea; Yes, exactly
> 2 Uhuh; What do you think?
> 3 I see; Yes, I know what you mean

DISCUSSION

9 👤 Remind the students of some of the historical places that were discussed at the start of the unit. Give students up to three minutes to take notes on one of the historical places they have visited.

10 👥 Students complete the task in small groups. Tell them to take it in turns to say just a few words about the place they have visited. The other group members should try to find out as much additional information as possible by asking questions.

Optional activity

You could turn Exercises 9 and 10 into a competitive game to be played in groups. For Exercise 9, ask each student to write down five bullet point notes on their historical place. For example, notes on Mount Rushmore could be:

1 It is in South Dakota, USA.

2 It features gigantic sculptures of the heads of four US presidents.

3 It was sculpted as a way of promoting tourism.

4 The original idea was to feature western heroes, not US presidents.

5 It was completed between 1927–1939.

The students should then get in to groups, but not show each other their notes. Each student takes a two-minute turn. During their turn, the student should briefly introduce the historical place. The other students then have to ask questions. If a student asks a question that can be answered from the notes, that student gets a point. When each student has taken a two-minute turn, the winner is the person who got the most points.

---

11 👥 Ask the students to get into groups of 3–5. If possible, students should each speak about a different historical place – so they should check which place each person will be talking about when forming their groups. Give each student a minute to explain to their group why their place is the most important. If two or more students have the same place, they should work together. The group then votes on the most important place. The vote should be based on how persuasive the arguments were, not just their own personal tastes.

⊙ LANGUAGE DEVELOPMENT

SYNONYMS

1 Ask the students to read the explanation box on synonyms and to find out why they are important. Elicit the answer from the class (they can help us avoid repeating the same word or phrase, and this helps us make what we say sound more interesting).

👤 Tell the students that the highlighted words can be divided in to two sets of synonyms: words similar to *army* and words similar to *discovered*. Ask the students to complete the two sets on their own. Quickly go through the answers with the class. With a stronger class, you could do this exercise as class work. However, there is a fair amount of text to process – so make sure that each student has time to read and understand the whole paragraph.

Answers
1 soldiers 2 found

2 👤 Students complete the task individually and check their answers in pairs. Quickly go through the answers with the class. Note that synonyms aren't always mutually replaceable. Here, *king* and *ruler* are used as variations of each other, but in other contexts this wouldn't be appropriate or possible.

Answers
1 ruler 2 young 3 plenty (of)

RELATIVE CLAUSES

Language note

There are two types of relative clause: *defining* (also called *identifying* or *restrictive*) and *non-defining* (also called *non-identifying* or *non-restrictive*).

Defining relative clauses make it clear what person or thing we are talking about (e.g. *The history book **which I borrowed from the library** was very useful*).

Non-defining relative clauses simply give us more information about the person or thing that we are talking about (e.g. *Tutankhamun, **who ruled Egypt 3,500 years ago**, died when he was 18*). This type of relative clause is more formal than defining relative clauses, and is not often used in normal speech.

As the listening exercise demonstrates, defining relative clauses follow immediately after the noun. They are not separated by commas when written down, and there is no pause or change of intonation in speech. Conversely, non-defining relative clauses are separated by commas in writing, and by pauses or changes in intonation when spoken.

It is important for your students to see and hear the difference between the two types of clause. This will help them sound more natural when speaking, and will also help them punctuate their sentences correctly.

---

3 👥 Students complete the task in pairs.

> **Answers**
> 1 a, c
> 2 b, d

4 (◀ 3.5) 👤 Students listen to the recording. Ask them to read the sentences as they listen, and notice the pauses at the commas.

5 👤👥 Students complete the task individually or in pairs.

> **Answers**
> 1 who 2 which 3 where (or in which) 4 which (or that)
> 5 who (or that) 6 where

6 👥 Students complete the task in pairs. Monitor the students as they take it in turns to say the sentences. You could finish off by modeling the sentences at random for the class to repeat, every now and again calling on a particular student to say the sentence alone.

LISTENING 2

PREPARING TO LISTEN

UNDERSTANDING KEY VOCABULARY

1 👤👥 Students complete the task individually and check their answers in pairs. Go through the answers with the class. Allow 3–5 minutes for the students to complete the task. If some students finish early, ask them to choose the three most useful new words for them, and to write down a sentence using each. You can check these sentences as you monitor one of the later activities.

> **Answers**
> 1 b founded c period
> 2 a defences b Middle Ages c protected
> 3 a Empire b ruled c took over

2 👥 Students complete the task in pairs. If you think that the students may not be sure of the answers, you could prompt them with very simple questions (e.g. *What countries do you know in the Middle East? What large cities do you know in the Middle East? What type of person usually has Roman numerals, e.g. II, after his or her name?*). Do not tell the class whether their answers are correct or not, as the answers will be revealed during the next task.

As an alternative to the above procedure, you could also do this task as a class exercise if you are fairly sure that at least one of the students will know the answers. If so, ask your students to close their books. You should then display a copy of the picture at the top of page 59 on an overhead projector. Ask the class what area is being displayed. If they tell you that it is the Middle East, ask them to focus on the shaded area and tell them that this is an empire that no longer exists. Elicit the term *Ottoman Empire* if possible, then ask the class questions 1–3. If one or more students seem particularly knowledgeable, encourage them to give more information (as long as this is likely to be interesting or useful to the rest of the class).

3 (◀ 3.6) 👤 Students listen and check their answers. Quickly go through the answers with the class.

> **Answers**
> 1 Algeria, Armenia, Azerbaijan, Bulgaria, Egypt, Greece, Iraq, Yemen
> (This is not an extensive list. At its height, the Ottoman Empire also included Albania, Bahrain, Bosnia and Herzegovina, Croatia, Cyprus, Eritrea, Georgia, Hungary, Iran, Israel, Jordan, Kosovo, Kuwait, Lebanon, Libya, Macedonia, Moldova, Montenegro, Oman, Qatar, Romania, Russia, Saudi Arabia, Serbia, Slovakia, Slovenia, Sudan, Syria, Tunisia, Turkey, the United Arab Emirates (UAE), Ukraine.)
> 2 Istanbul
> 3 A sultan (ruler) of the Ottoman Empire – a military ruler

WHILE LISTENING

LISTENING FOR DETAIL

4 (◀ 3.7) 👥 Ask the students to go through the questions in pairs and try to guess whether the answers are true or false. Even if they have no idea, they should still decide on an answer. This will help make sure that they have read and understood the questions before listening to the recording. You could then elicit the answers from the class, but do not confirm whether or not they are correct. The students should then listen to the recording and check their answers. Quickly go through the answers with the class.

> **Answers**
> 1 F 2 T 3 T 4 F

5 (🔊 3.7) 👤 Before you play the recording a second time, first ask the students to try and complete the notes individually from memory. Set a strict time limit of two minutes, then play the recording a second time. The students should check their ideas and complete any remaining gaps. Quickly go elicit the answers from the class.

> **Answers**
>
> 1432 – Mehmed II born
> 1453 – captured Constantinople
> 53 days to take over the city
> – hired engineers to develop modern weapons
> he broke the city walls
> – after taking over the city – moved the capital to Constantinople
> – rebuilt the city – univs. and colleges
> – invited edu. men to live in the city
> 1451–1481 – ruled the Ottoman Empire
> 1481 – Mehmed died
> Constantinople = Istanbul (capital until 1922)

Optional activity

Write this abbreviation on the board: *e.g.* Tell the students that it is a well-known abbreviation, and is common in both formal writing and in note-taking. Ask the students what it means (*for example*). Then write this on the board: *yrs.* Tell the students that this abbreviation is often used in note-taking, and ask them to guess what it means (*years*). Then ask the class to identify the two abbreviations in the notes and to tell you what the full forms are. The two abbreviations are *univs.* (*universities*) and *edu.* (*educated*). Ask the students how they can tell that these are abbreviations (they have a full-stop after them, and are not complete words).

POST-LISTENING

LISTENING FOR TEXT ORGANIZATION FEATURES

Language note

When we describe events from the past, we often use sequence words (*next, then, finally,* etc.). These words help listeners understand the order that events happened.

---

6 Allow up to two minutes for the students to complete the task individually and then check their answers in pairs. Point out that the first question has been done as an example. Quickly go through the answers with the class

> **Answers**
>
> 2 During 3 After that 4 Meanwhile 5 Eventually

DISCUSSION

7 👤 Students complete the task individually. Set a strict time limit of two minutes, or 90 seconds for a stronger class.

8 👥 Students complete the task in small groups. Tell the students that they should each talk for a minute, and that the person to their left should ask them a question related to their topic. The student should then answer the question and invite further questions from the rest of the group. The groups should repeat this procedure until everyone has explained their ideas.

CRITICAL THINKING

ANALYZE

1 👤 Tell the students to quickly underline the facts individually. Elicit the answers from the class. You could first ask them how many facts they have found. There may be some differences of opinion as to what constitutes a single 'fact'. For example, some may say that *at 21 he led an army of 200,000 men and 320 ships to take over the city of Constantinople* is one fact, some may say two and some may say three.

> **Answers**
>
> He was sometimes referred to as 'Mehmed the Conqueror'
> He was born in 1432
> At the age of 21, he led an army of 200,000 men and 320 ships to take over the city of Constantinople

2 👤 Students complete the task individually and check their answers in pairs. Elicit the answers from the students. You could first ask how many of the opinions are given (two).

> **Answers**
> b, c

Optional activity

It is quite common for students to offer contentious opinions as fact. It is important to find ways of getting them to understand the difference between fact and opinion, to be able to identify the two when they read articles or watch TV and to be able to distinguish between fact and opinion during their own writing and discussion work.

Tell students that they are going to do some critical thinking work in the area of fact and opinion. Ask them to write down six facts individually. They should then work in small groups and read their facts out.

The other students should decide whether each fact is indeed a fact, or whether it is an opinion. Where the group agree that an opinion has been given instead of a fact, they should try to rewrite the (subjective) opinion as an (objective) fact. Tell them to be ready to give feedback on the activity to the class. Give the students 3–5 minutes to discuss their facts, then ask each group in turn if any of the 'facts' were actually opinions. This may give rise to some interesting discussion. When you have got feedback from each group, ask the groups to discuss the difference between facts and opinions, and why it is important to be able to distinguish the two. Give the students another minute or so to discuss this, then lead a class feedback session.

3 👥 Students complete the task in pairs. Quickly go through the answers with the class.

> **Answers**
> 1 O 2 F 3 F 4 O 5 O 6 F

The first statement (*Mehmed II is the most famous ruler in history*) could be seen as a *incorrect* statement of fact, rather than an opinion. Your students might try to argue that someone either is 'the most famous' or they aren't (although it would be extremely difficult to establish whether or not one particular historical person is really the 'most famous'. Conversely, whether or not a ruler is 'the greatest' is more clearly a matter of opinion. If this issue is raised by your students, you could ask them to change the words 'most famous' to 'greatest' and then ask them whether the statement is one of fact or opinion.

CREATE

4 👤👥 Students complete the task individually or in pairs. With a stronger class, have the students complete the task individually. You could ask them to try and think of a person that might not be immediately obvious to the rest of the class, this would help avoid too many students choosing the same person. If your students are struggling to think of how to complete the *why?* section, ask them to think of one famous event that their historical figure was involved in, or a decision that the person took, and why they acted as they did.

5 👤👥 Students complete the task individually or in pairs. With a stronger class, have the students complete the task individually. Point

out that the opinions could be either broadly critical of the fact or broadly in favour (for or against). To encourage the students to analyze the facts from different perspectives, you could ask them to write at least one opinion for and one opinion against each fact. You could model this by saying the following (or similar).

Fact: Neil Armstrong was the first person on the moon.

Opinion for: Putting someone on the moon was important for our knowledge of space.

Opinion against: Putting someone on the moon was a waste of money; the money could have been spent helping poor people.

6 👥 Students complete the task in pairs.

EVALUATE

7 👥 Ask students to form new pairs, so that each student is sitting with someone new. The students then take it in turns in their pairs to discuss the questions. Give the students two minutes each to answer questions 1–3. When the time has elapsed, tell the first student in each pair to quickly finish off so that their partner can begin their turn. Give the pairs another two minutes. Finish off by quickly asking each student who their first partner talked about, and what was the most interesting fact they learned or opinion they heard.

SPEAKING

PREPARATION FOR SPEAKING

TALKING ABOUT PAST EVENTS

> **Optional activity**
>
> Ask the class to close their books. Then tell them that they are going to read about an explorer, and that they should try to guess who that explorer might be. Elicit from the class the names of some famous explorers. If they can't think of any, then you could widen the question to include adventurers in general (both from history and fictional). Elicit one or two facts about each one, plus one opinion.
>
> The explorer in the text may not be as well known as some others, so your students may not guess the name. This is fine – the purpose of this introductory activity is to focus the students' attention on the topic, not to find out how much they know about different explorers.

1 (◀) 3.8 ⚫ Give the students up to five minutes to complete the task. When most of the class seem to be ready, ask them to quickly complete or check their tables with a partner.

Answers

regular verbs	irregular verbs
travelled	did
crossed	were
visited	was
lasted	went
returned	took
missed	set off
described	left
died	wrote
helped	saw

PRONUNCIATION FOR SPEAKING

2 ⚫ Students complete the task individually. They will have the chance to discuss the pronunciation further in Exercise 3.

3 (◀) 3.9 ⚫⚫ ⚫⚫⚫ Students listen to the recording and complete the task in pairs or small groups. Tell them that they must all agree on the correct pronunciation of each -ed ending. Give them 2–3 minutes to discuss the pronunciation. Quickly find out from each group whether or not they all agree on the correct pronunciation. If there is disagreement, play the recording again.

Answers

travelled /ɪd/   missed /t/
crossed /t/   described /d/
visited /ɪd/   died /d/
lasted /ɪd/   helped /t/
returned /d/

TALKING ABOUT TIME

4 ⚫ Give the students 2–3 minutes to complete the task individually. You could point out that questions 1–12 includes both synonyms and definitions, and that some of the answers include short phrases and not only one word synonyms. When most of the class is ready, ask the students to quickly compare their answers with a partner.

Answers

2 century 3 medieval 4 then 5 the 1300s 6 at the age of 7 at that time 8 a short while later 9 recent 10 late 11 mid 12 early

5 ⚫⚫ ⚫⚫⚫ Ask the students to read the language notes on the different ways of saying years. Then give them up to two minutes to say the sentences out loud in small groups. Quickly elicit the correct pronunciation of the sentences from the class, calling on students at random. If a student does not say the sentence correctly, model the sentence and ask the student to repeat it. If the student is still struggling, get the whole class to say the sentence and then call on a different student.

6 ⚫⚫ Ask the students to read the opinions on being a confident speaker. Quickly elicit from the class situations in which they have had to speak publicly. How did they feel? How did it go? How would they feel now about speaking in public? Give the students 3–5 minutes to discuss the task. Tell them to think of a piece of useful advice for each situation.

Optional activity

Ask students to read each of the opinions (a–d), and to ask which one of those (if any) most applies to them. Assign one of the situations to each corner of the room, and ask the students to go to the appropriate corner. Students who are unable to decide which situation most applies to them, or to whom none of the situations apply, should go to the centre. Then give each group up to five minutes to discuss how these situations apply to them (in the case of those students in the four corners) and what they can do to overcome the problem. Ask them to try and think of at least 3–5 specific pieces of advice. The students in the centre of the room should discuss each of the situations in more general terms, and think of at least one specific piece of advice for each one.

7 ⚫⚫⚫ Students complete the task in small groups. If you have done the optional activity for Exercise 6, you may skip this task.

SPEAKING TASK

PREPARE

1 ⚫ Give the students a strict time limit of three minutes to write short notes on 3–5 historical figures or events. Tell them that their notes should include information about both men and women. Alternatively, you could tell the male members of the group to take notes about women only (or about events that largely concerned women, or in which women played an important role), and the women to take notes about men (or about events that largely involved men).

2 Students complete the task in small groups. Give them 3–5 minutes to share their ideas and to decide on which topic would be the most interesting.

3 Give the students 5–10 minutes to complete the task individually and to prepare a five-minute presentation. Tell them to take notes, rather than writing full sentences. This will help make the presentation feel more natural. Tell them that the presentations should be fairly informal and conversational rather than overly formal and rehearsed. You could say that students more used to public speaking could give a more formal presentation if they want, but that the key to this task is to keep things interesting for the audience.

PRACTISE

4 Students complete the task in pairs. Allow up to 15 minutes: five minutes for each presentation and roughly two minutes for feedback and discussion following each presentation. To make the final presentations tighter, you could tell the students that the second version of their presentations should only be four minutes long (rather than five) and that during this practice stage, they should also give the following feedback: *What would I have liked to have heard more about? What information could be left out?*

PRESENT

5 Students complete the task in small groups. Tell them that they have a strict time limit of four minutes, and that you will warn them when they have only one minute left. This will help keep the presentations tighter, and will encourage the groups to complete the task at roughly the same time. You could also give the students up to a minute to answer any questions. To ensure that there are some questions, and to encourage the students to listen to each other's presentation, you could say that following each presentation, the person to the left of the speaker must ask a question related to the talk.

TASK CHECKLIST AND OBJECTIVES REVIEW

Refer students to the end of each unit for the Task checklist and Objectives review. Students complete the tables individually to reflect on their learning and identify areas for improvement.

WORDLIST

See Teaching tips, pages 9–11 for ideas about how to make the most of the Wordlist with your students.

REVIEW TEST

See pages 102–103 for the photocopiable Review test for this unit, and page 91 for ideas about when and how to administer the Review test.

ADDITIONAL SPEAKING TASK

See page 120 for an Additional speaking task related to this unit.

Put students in groups of three. Focus them on the topic of the discussion and ask them to read about their individual roles (A, B or C). Allow them one or two minutes to prepare and make notes. Then ask them to discuss the topic. Allow up to 10 minutes for the interaction, then ask them to report back to the whole class about what they discussed.

RESEARCH PROJECT

Create an audio story about a famous person in history.

Explain to your students that they will be writing a story about a famous person from the past. Ask them to think about someone outside their own country. They should research where that person was born, their nationality, their early life and why they were famous. Students could use the blog in the Cambridge LMS to show what they have learnt.

Students will write a story about their chosen famous person and record this as an audio file. They can add music and sound effects (search for 'free sound effects'). The story can then be uploaded to the forum on the Cambridge LMS for other students to listen to (audio recordings should be saved as 128kb mp3 files). Students could also write a task for other members of the class to complete based on their audio story.

4 TRANSPORT

UNLOCK YOUR KNOWLEDGE

👥 Allow 4–5 minutes for students to discuss the questions in pairs and then invite feedback from the class. Select one pair and ask them for a summary of their responses.

WATCH AND LISTEN

▶ Video script

How can you make an environmentally friendly car that still drives at fast speeds? Cars that run on diesel fuel rather than petrol are often considered dirty and old-fashioned.

However, German car-maker BMW has developed the technology to make diesel engines cleaner, bringing them into the 21st century.

Old diesel engines were made of iron and were very heavy, but the new BMW engine cases are made of aluminium and are 40% lighter. This makes their cars much more efficient, as they can travel further on less fuel.

The BMW factory in Austria makes 700,000 engines a year, but the engines are fitted inside the cars five hours away in Germany.

The BMW factory in Germany is one of the most modern in the world. Almost every process is automated.

The cars are assembled by huge robots.

This is the exhaust unit.

The engine and exhaust are added to the chassis and suspension. Robot carts take them to the final part of the factory line.

At this stage, the engine is combined with the body of the car. This only takes 80 seconds. The BMW factory can produce 44 cars an hour.

The last part of the process is attaching the badge to the finished car.

BMW cars can reach speeds of up to 270 kilometres per hour. Through a combination of modern technology and high power, the company ensures that their cars are some of the fastest and cleanest on the road.

PREPARING TO WATCH

USING KEY VOCABULARY

1 👤 Students complete the task individually and check their answers in pairs. Tell the students to underline or highlight the most useful new phrases, and to record these in their vocabulary books.

Answers

1 environmentally friendly cars
2 run on diesel fuel
3 considered to be old-fashioned
4 fuel-efficient cars
5 aluminium cases
6 engines are fitted inside
7 robotic arms
8 reach speeds of up to

PREDICTING CONTENT

2 👥 Give the students a few minutes to discuss the task in pairs, then elicit ideas from the class. Encourage students to support their ideas with evidence from the photographs and sentences.

3 ▶👤 Students watch the video and check their answers to Exercise 2.

Answers

1 The video is about the production of BMW cars.
2 It focuses on new, environmentally friendly diesel engines.
3 The video suggests that cars that run on diesel fuel rather than petrol are often considered dirty and old-fashioned.

WHILE WATCHING

UNDERSTANDING MAIN IDEAS

4 Students complete the task individually and compare their answers in pairs. With stronger groups, you could ask them first to try to answer the questions from memory before watching the video again to check and complete their answers. Quickly elicit the answers from the class.

> **Answers**
> 1 a 2 b 3 c

UNDERSTANDING DETAIL

5 ▶ Students complete the task individually and compare their answers in pairs. Again, with stronger groups, you could ask them first to try to answer the questions from memory before watching the video again to check and complete their answers. Quickly elicit the answers from the class.

> **Answers**
> 1 40% 2 700,000 3 44 4 270

DISCUSSION

6 Give the students 30 seconds to rank the features individually.

7 Students complete the task in small groups. Tell them to agree on a group ranking. Where there is strong disagreement, each student should say why they think that the feature in question is or isn't especially important, or should be given a particular position in the list. Give students a few minutes to decide on a common ranking, then elicit the top and bottom two features from each group. You could try to get the class to agree on the top three, encouraging discussion where there is disagreement.

LISTENING 1

PRONUNCIATION FOR LISTENING

> **Optional activity**
>
> Write these words on the board.
>
> *fast, quickly, make, passenger, use*
>
> Tell the class that *fast* is an adjective. Then ask the class what type of word each of the others is. The last word is *use*. Your students will probably correctly identify it as a verb, but may not be so quick in realizing that it is also a noun. If the students only identify one of the two possible parts of speech, try to elicit the other by saying *Yes, it's a verb. But is that all?* When you have elicited the fact that *use* is both a verb and a noun, ask your students in pairs to think of a sentence illustrating each use. Ask them to repeat their sentences to each other, and to notice the difference in pronunciation. Monitor the class as they do this, giving feedback as appropriate. Note one pair that have a good set of sentences that are correctly pronounced. Give the students a minute or so to write and repeat their sentences, then call on one pair to say their sentences to the class. Establish that *use* as a verb is pronounced /juːz/, whereas as a noun it is pronounced /juːs/. Tell the class that although some words have the same form when they are a noun or a verb, the pronunciation is often different.
>
> *fast* (most frequently an adjective, although it can also be a verb or a noun)
> *quickly* (adverb)
> *make* (verb, although it can also be a noun)
> *passenger* (noun)
> *use* (verb and noun)

1 ◀) 4.1 Students complete the task individually. You could ask them to try and answer the questions in pairs first and then check their answers against the recording.

> **Answers**
> a 2 b 1 c re<u>search</u> (verb); <u>research</u> (noun)

2 ◀) 4.2 Students complete the task individually. Again, you could ask them to answer the questions in pairs first and check their answers against the recording.

> **Answers**
> 1 <u>research</u> 2 re<u>search</u>ing 3 de<u>creased</u> 4 <u>decrease</u>
> 5 pre<u>sented</u> 6 <u>present</u> 7 <u>transport</u> 8 trans<u>port</u>

3 👥 Give the students up to two minutes to practise saying the sentences in small groups.

PREPARING TO LISTEN

UNDERSTANDING KEY VOCABULARY

4 👤 Give the students three minutes to complete the task individually and then check their answers in pairs.

> **Answers**
>
> 1 d 2 g 3 b 4 e 5 f 6 c 7 h 8 a 9 j 10 i

USING YOUR KNOWLEDGE

5 👥 Give the students five minutes to discuss their ideas in small groups, and tell each group to be ready to provide a brief summary of the ideas discussed. As three of the four questions concern plane travel, tell the class that those students who have never flown should instead describe the longest trip that they have even taken by some other means of transport. Elicit one or two short anecdotes from each group, then lead a brief class discussion to find out which form of transport the students think is the most dangerous. If there is much disagreement, encourage further discussion by asking the students to support their ideas with examples, stories or other information that they might have. If the class have internet access, you could give them a few minutes to quickly research the topic online and to find out which form of transport is the most dangerous statistically, either in their own country or worldwide). The answer to which form of transport is the most dangerous will be answered in the next listening task.

WHILE LISTENING

LISTENING FOR MAIN IDEAS

6 🔊 **4.3** 👤 Students complete the task individually. With a weaker group, or if the vocabulary is likely to be problematic, you could ask the students to read the questions and to try to guess the answers before listening to the recording. If so, the students should then check their answers against the recording.

> **Answers**
>
> 1 b 2 a 3 a 4 c

LISTENING FOR DETAIL

7 👥 Students complete the task in pairs. You could also ask them to discuss any other ideas they have on how to reduce a fear of flying. Give the students a few minutes to discuss their ideas, then quickly establish with the class which tip most people think is the most useful. You could also ask whether anyone has overcome their own fear of flying, and how they were able to do this.

8 🔊 **4.4** 👤 Students complete the task individually. Quickly go through the answers with the class.

> **Answers**
>
> 1, 4, 6

9 👤 Students complete the task individually. You could set this up competitively, and tell the students to complete the summary as fast as possible and to raise a hand once complete. Once the first student has raised their hand, tell the class that they have 30 seconds to complete the text. Tell the student who first completed the text to quickly check their work to make sure that all of the words are in the right place. Then ask that student to read the whole text aloud. If they make an error, tell them to stop and invite another student to take over – starting with the correct word. Continue like this until you have gone through the whole text.

10 🔊 **4.4** Play the recording again for students to check their answers.

> **Answers**
>
> 1 reduce 2 engine 3 wings 4 normal 5 damaged
> 6 avoid 7 flying 8 driving

POST-LISTENING

> **Optional activity**
>
> Ask students to read the information box and to discuss in pairs or small groups the kinds of situations in which rhetorical questions are useful. Elicit ideas from the class. These may include (among others) political speeches, advertising, debates and presentations. More generally, some of the uses of rhetorical questions include entertaining, persuading, informing, educating, shocking, and calling people to take action.

11 (◀) **4.3** 👤 Students complete the task individually. Quickly go through the answers with the class.

> **Answers**
>
> 1, 2, 3, 6 are rhetorical questions

> **Optional activity**
>
> Put students into pairs. Give each pair a random object that you have nearby, such as a pen, paper clip, cup, glass, board rubber, mobile phone or a mouse, etc. Give each pair 5–10 minutes to write and rehearse a short radio advertisement for the object. Tell the students that the advert must include at least one rhetorical question. Monitor the class as they write and rehearse their advertisements, giving feedback as appropriate. Then ask each pair to perform their advertisement while the rest of the class try to identify the rhetorical question(s). You could play them one or two short radio advertisements to give them an idea of the kind of language that is used on the radio. You can find examples of radio and TV advertisements that include rhetorical questions online by typing *advertisements with rhetorical questions* into your search engine.

DISCUSSION

12 👥👥 Ask the students to look at the picture of the spider. Then ask them to close their books and to quickly share with a partner how they feel when they see spiders. Ask them if they know the word that means fear of spiders (arachnophobia). Then ask them to get into groups of 3–5 and give them 3–5 minutes to discuss the questions. Tell them that they can also discuss their own fears if they wish. If so, they should decide with the group whether these personal fears are normal, or whether they are so extreme that they could be described as a phobia. When the students have finished their discussions, quickly elicit one or two ideas from each group.

⊙ LANGUAGE DEVELOPMENT

TALKING ABOUT ACHIEVEMENT

1 👤 Students complete the task individually and check their answers in pairs.

> **Answers**
>
> b concentrate c method d control e challenge
> f goal g relax h get over i completed j positive

> **Optional activity**
>
> You could point out one or two of the collocations in sentences 1–8, and then ask the students to identify the others. If your students are not sure what a collocation is, give this example from the text (e.g. the *right attitude*) and tell them that a collocation is the combination of words formed when two or more words are often used together in a way that sounds correct.
>
> Examples of collocations from the text include: *right attitude, stay positive, long time,* and *emergency exit*. Point out that it is useful to highlight these combinations of words when they read texts, as it will help them to use English more naturally.

2 👥👥 Ask the students to work with a new partner, and give them 2–4 minutes to discuss the questions. If you feel comfortable talking about yourself in class, you could set this task up by giving your own (brief) answers to one or more of the questions. Ask the class if anyone heard about any unusual achievements or goals. Give some of the students the opportunity to briefly outline some of the things they heard, then go on to the next task. If you have time, you could try to establish what the most common goals are, and what advice students have to help their peers stay positive when faced with challenges.

COMPARING THINGS

3 (◀) **4.5** 👤 Students complete the task individually and compare their answers in pairs. You could ask them to try and answer the questions in pairs first and then check their answers against the recording. Quickly elicit the answers from the students.

> **Answers**
>
> 2 far; dangerous 3 considerably 4 much 5 definitely

4 👥👥 Students complete the task in pairs. If you think that the students may find this task challenging, have them work in small groups rather than in pairs.

> **Answers**
>
> 1 sentences 1, 3, 4, 5
> 2 sentence 2
> 3 1 a lot 2 by far 3 considerably 4 much 5 definitely
> 4 they all mean 'very much' or 'a lot'

5 👤 Students complete the task individually and compare their answers in pairs. You could do the first one with the class as an example; this may help remind them that the correct form (in this case, *better*) may be very different to the adjectives in brackets (in this case, *good*).

> **Answers**
>
> 1 better 2 faster 3 most comfortable 4 better
> 5 most interesting 6 more convenient 7 best

6 👤 Give the students a few minutes to complete the task individually. Monitor the students as they work, giving feedback as appropriate. When the students seem to be finishing off, ask them to quickly finish the question they are working on and to get together with a new partner.

7 👥 Students complete the task in pairs. This could generate a lot of useful discussion, so allow up to five minutes for this task. Monitor the students during the discussion and take notes on their use of language (both correct and incorrect). When the students have finished their discussions, give some examples of some of the especially good language that you heard. Pick out some of the typical errors that students are making (in grammar, vocabulary and pronunciation) and elicit corrections from the class where possible.

LISTENING 2

PREPARING TO LISTEN

UNDERSTANDING KEY VOCABULARY

1 👤 Students complete the task individually and compare their answers in pairs. Quickly go through the answers with the class.

> **Answers**
>
> 1 experience 2 hit 3 convenience 4 overtake
> 5 injured 6 respect 7 heavy fine 8 lanes
> 9 break the law 10 prevent

USING YOUR KNOWLEDGE

2 👥 Students discuss the questions in pairs. You could also ask them to think of some solutions to the disadvantages (e.g. *cycling to work can make you sweaty, so employers should provide showers*). Give the students a few minutes to discuss the questions, then elicit suggestions from the class.

WHILE LISTENING

LISTENING FOR MAIN IDEAS

3 ◀) 4.6 👥👤 Ask the students to read the list of options and agree with a partner on the most likely answers. They should then listen to the recording, complete the task individually and compare their answers in pairs. Quickly go through the answers with the class.

> **Answers**
>
> 1, 3, 5, 6, 7, 8 (the answers are given in a different order in the recording)

LISTENING FOR DETAIL

4 ◀) 4.6 👤👥 Play the recording again. Students complete the task individually or in pairs. Quickly elicit the answers from the class.

> **Answers**
>
> 1 a, c
> 2 b, d
> 3 a, c
> 4 a, d

5 ◀) 4.7 👥👤 Ask students to read through the notes in pairs and to think of likely words or phrases that could be used to complete the gaps. Elicit some ideas from the class, but avoid commenting at this stage. Play the recording and ask the class to check their ideas and complete the gaps according to the interview. After the recording has finished, give the students a few more moments to complete the gaps and then go through the answers with the class.

> **Answers**
>
> 1 wider 2 separate 3 fines

POST-LISTENING

LISTENING FOR TEXT ORGANIZATION FEATURES

6 (◀ 4.7) 👤 Students complete the task individually. Quickly go through the answers with the class.

> **Answers**
> 1, 3, 4, 6, 7

7 👥 👥👥 Ask the students to discuss, in pairs or small groups, their own experiences of cycling in their city. Students that have not cycled much should talk about someone they know who has. The students should then discuss what could be done to improve things for cyclists in their city. Encourage the students to use language from Exercise 6. Encourage them to learn and use the phrases that they feel most comfortable with. This will help them sound more natural during the discussion task. Give the students 2–4 minutes to discuss the question. Monitor the groups and give feedback during and after the exercise as appropriate.

DISCUSSION

8 👤 Give the students up to three minutes to take notes on the questions. If you have time, and the students have access to the internet, you could give them a few minutes extra to research the topic online.

9 👥👥👥 Students complete the task in groups. Appoint a chair and a secretary for each group, ideally students who have not yet spoken much during the class. The chair should start the meeting and confirm its aims. They should then ensure that everyone gets an equal chance to put forward their views. The secretary should take notes on what is said, and is responsible for correctly noting down the three proposals agreed upon. Give the students up to 10 minutes to complete the task, then invite the secretaries to outline the groups' proposals. When the secretaries outline their proposals, you could make short notes on the board. The class should then decide on the best three proposals. If there is no clear consensus, you could tell the students that they are each allowed three votes. One student per proposal should then quickly outline why their proposals should be carried forward. The class can then vote with a show

of hands. Repeat this procedure until all of the proposals have been voted on.

> ## Optional activity
>
> If the class have voted on the best three proposals, you could divide the class into three groups and tell them to further develop the proposal. What exactly would be involved? What other considerations might there be? Which interested parties should be consulted? How much might the proposal cost if carried out? What research must be carried out in order to present a more detailed proposal? Tell each group that they must research the proposal in more detail for the next class using English language websites (as far as possible). They must then present the more detailed outline of the proposal during the next class. Give the groups 5–10 minutes to finalize their proposal at the start of the next class, then invite each group to present their ideas in under five minutes. Once each proposal has been presented, the class should vote on which was the best. Give each student two votes (to avoid the problem of them voting for their own proposal).

CRITICAL THINKING

ANALYZE

1 👤 Ask students to quickly read through the list and to tell you which of the two actions are carried out by pedestrians rather than by drivers (3 and 8). If necessary, explain that *jaywalking* is the action of crossing a street unlawfully. Then ask students to go through the list again and to decide which of the actions are illegal in their country. If they are unsure of the answers, you could ask them to research the questions online as a homework task and to report back during the next class.

2 👥👥 Students complete the task in pairs. You could ask them to rank them in order. Give the students 2–3 minutes to decide on the order, and encourage them to discuss the reasons behind their decisions (e.g. *Most people listen to music while driving, so I don't think that it can be very dangerous*). You could quickly establish with the class which one action they think is the most dangerous, and which is the least dangerous.

3 Ask the students to quickly read through the report. Elicit reactions from students showing obvious signs of surprise (if none do, then call on two or three students at random). Ask the students to explain why they are/are not surprised by the report. You could point out that *texting* refers to sending (sms) text messages using a mobile phone.

APPLY

4 👤 Give the students two minutes to take notes on the question. Tell them to assume that the question refers to the use of handheld mobile phones, and not to using hands-free technology to make calls or send texts.

5 👥 Ask students to form new groups and to first discuss their own attitude towards doing this. Is this illegal? If so, what are the possible punishments? If not, should it be? Give the students a few minutes to discuss their own ideas, then elicit a quick summary from each group. The groups should then discuss their ides for solving the problem. Allow up to five minutes for further discussion, then ask each group to report back to the class.

SPEAKING

PREPARATION FOR SPEAKING

1 🔊 4.8 👥 Ask the class to read the information box. Then ask them to listen to the recording and discuss the ideas presented in pairs. Quickly elicit the most popular opinions from the class. You could also ask the students whether they have any other ideas as to how to deal with the problem of eating while driving.

2 👤👥 Students complete the task individually or in pairs. Quickly elicit the answers from the class.

> **Answers**
> 2 I think it would be better if
> 3 I think it would be much better if
> 4 The best thing would be to

> **Language note**
> The conjunction *that* is often missed out in these phrases.
> 1 I don't think **(that)** the government should do anything about it.
> 2 I think **(that)** it would be better if they closed drive-through restaurants.
> 3 I think **(that)** it would be much better if drivers weren't allowed to eat or drink while they drive.
> If your students ask you why *that* is missing, you can tell them that this is a common feature of relatively informal speaking and writing.

3 👤👥 Students complete the task individually or in pairs. Quickly elicit the answers from the class.

> **Answers**
> a 3 b 1 c 4 d 2

4 👤👥 Students complete the task individually or in pairs. Quickly elicit the answers from the class. Alternatively, simply elicit the answers directly from the class.

> **Answers**
> talking about a personal experience: *From my own experience*; *Personally* giving a reason: *the reason for this is*; *this is because*

> **Optional activity**
> 👤👥 Ask students to read the explanation box. Then give them a strict time limit of two minutes to quickly write down four examples from their own lives (using the Past simple, Past continuous, Present perfect and a sentence including *never*). The students should then go through these with a partner to check that they are all correct. Each partner should then ask one follow-up question for each sentence. Allow 3–5 minutes for discussion, then elicit examples from the class.

5 👤 Students complete the task individually and compare their answers in pairs. Quickly go through the answers with the class.

> **Answers**
> 1 have; eaten 2 went 3 have had (*had* is also possible)
> 4 Have; (ever) travelled 5 had 6 have; seen
> 7 was driving; rang

6 👥 Give the students up to five minutes to complete the task. Quickly elicit any particularly interesting examples from the class. Was anyone surprised by what they learned about their partner?

SPEAKING TASK

PREPARE

1 🔊 4.9 👤 Ask the class whether or not they text and walk. Then play the recording and elicit from the class whether or not they think that it is dangerous to text and walk. Elicit examples of the kinds of accidents that can happen from the class. You could point out that some smartphone apps have been designed that use the camera to display what is happening in front of the person texting on their screen display. Have they ever used such an app? Would such an app be useful?

2 👥 Put the students into groups of four. Either allocate roles or ask them to decide on these with the group. Give them a minute to read and understand their roles. Tell the students to really learn the roles, so that they do not have to refer to the card. Ask them to try and become that person as far as possible. What is the person's name? What are their hopes, dreams or fears? This may sound a little over the top, but it will help to create a light atmosphere and ease people into their roles, some of which may include ideas and attitudes very different to the students' own. Then give them up to five minutes to do the role-play. Monitor the groups and give feedback at the end. There is no real need to elicit ideas or summaries at the end of this task, as each group will have heard similar arguments and attitudes.

PRACTISE

3 👥 Give the students two minutes to complete the task in pairs. Two minutes will be enough, as each partner will be playing the same role and will have similar ideas.

DISCUSS

4 👥 Ask students to form new groups of four. Students should not be working with anyone from Exercise 2. As they have already discussed these questions twice in their roles, you could tell them to discuss their own ideas – rather than those written on their role cards. Give them 3–5 minutes to discuss their opinions and to suggest some concrete solutions. Be careful not to let this speaking task last for too long, as the students will have already discussed the topic at some length. Quickly elicit suggestions from the class, reminding them that they only need make suggestions that have not already been put forward.

TASK CHECKLIST AND OBJECTIVES REVIEW

Refer students to the end of each unit for the Task checklist and Objectives review. Students complete the tables individually to reflect on their learning and identify areas for improvement.

WORDLIST

See Teaching tips, pages 9–11 for ideas about how to make the most of the Wordlist with your students.

REVIEW TEST

See pages 104–105 for the photocopiable Review test for this unit, and page 91 for ideas about when and how to administer the Review test.

ADDITIONAL SPEAKING TASK

See page 121 for an Additional speaking task related to this unit.

Put students in groups of four. Focus them on the discussion topic and their role card (A, B, C or D). Allow up to two minutes for them to make notes, and then ask them to begin their discussion. Give 10 minutes for the discussion, and then ask each group to report their opinions to the whole class.

RESEARCH PROJECT

Create a presentation to show how a car is made.

Divide the class into groups and ask them to brainstorm how they think cars are made. Ask students to think about materials, processes and design. Then ask them to search 'how cars are made'. Students can use tools on the wiki on the Cambridge LMS as a central place to share information on this topic.

When students have researched the different stages, ask them to use presentation software to create a presentation including pictures, narration, sound effects and music. The class can then vote for the best presentation, based on how clear it is, how interesting it is and the quality of information presented. There are free online voting systems which allow you to do this. Search for 'voting software' to view some of these.

Learning objectives

Before you start the *Unlock your knowledge* section, ask students to read the Learning objectives box. This will give them a clear idea of what they will learn in the unit. Tell them that you will return to these objectives at the end of the unit, when they review what they have learned. Give students the opportunity to ask any questions they might have.

UNLOCK YOUR KNOWLEDGE

Background note

The photo shows a range of solar panels, which collect and generate energy from sunlight.

Optional lead in

👥 👥👥 Start the class by asking how the country produces its energy. For example, does it use mainly fossil fuels (such as oil, coal and gas)? Elicit ideas from the class and take notes on the board. On the left-hand side, write down any suggestions as to traditional sources (but do not label the list) and on the right-hand side write down any alternative forms suggested (again, do not label the list). Once the class have given you all of their ideas, ask them to look at the list and to tell you what each side of the board represents (if you only have notes on one side of the board, add one or two ideas of your own on the other side). Elicit the answer from the board. Then ask the class to discuss in pairs or small groups whether the question of sourcing energy is an issue in their country. Allow a minute for discussion, then elicit ideas from the class.

As a follow-up task, you could find images online using your search engine. Run a search on 'energy sources' and scroll through the different pictures using a digital projector. As you do so, elicit the different types of energy sources displayed and ask the class whether they are considered traditional or alternative.

👥👥👥 Students discuss questions 1–3 in small groups. Give the students up to three minutes, then quickly elicit suggestions from some of the groups. You could finish off by asking the class whether or not their country is too dependent on traditional sources of energy, and what the consequences of this might be in both the short and long term. If the country exports fossil fuels, what might the long-term effects of an increased use of alternative energy across the world be?

WATCH AND LISTEN

▶ Video script

In the east of Russia, nine hours from Moscow, lies one of the most active volcanic regions on earth: Kamchatka. The Kamchatka region is as big as California, but only 400,000 people live there, surrounded by 300 volcanic sites.

Volcanologist Sasha Ovsyannikov has worked in the volcanoes of Kamchatka for 35 years.

Among the most active volcanoes in the region is Mutnovsky. It was formed 45,000 years ago when four smaller volcanoes collapsed, into one vast volcano cone. It is 1.5km across.

Sasha is checking the activity in the volcano. It could explode at any moment, releasing dangerous clouds of ash and gas into the air. But Sasha feels no fear.

"You cannot help but fall in love with volcanoes because they are like living things. They live their own lives and each erupts in its own way. Like people, volcanoes are all different"

He takes samples of rock and gas from the volcano to see whether Mutnovsky is about to erupt. Sasha works with scientists at a volcano institute. They check Sasha's rock samples and monitor the 19 big volcanoes in the region and try to predict the next eruption.

The volcanoes of Kamchatka are a threat to the aircraft that cross the region. Ash from an eruption can rise 14km above the ground and travel thousands of kilometres. The rock and dust in the ash can damage a plane's engine and cause it to crash.

Sasha and his colleague fly to another volcano 100km away, called Karymsky, to investigate how active it is. When they arrive, everything seems calm, but suddenly, without warning, Karymsky erupts. An explosion of this size is very unusual. A week later, Sasha and his pilot decide it is safe enough to fly over the crater of Karymsky.

Thanks to the work of Sasha and other scientists, the world's airlines will be warned immediately if Karymsky, or any other volcanoes in Kamchatka, are likely to explode again soon.

PREPARING TO WATCH

UNDERSTANDING KEY VOCABULARY

1 👤 Students complete the task individually and check their answers in pairs. Quickly go through the answers with the students.

> Answers
> 1 c 2 a 3 d 4 e 5 f 6 b 7 h 8 g

2 👥 Give the students two minutes to complete the task in pairs. Elicit the answers from the class.

> **Answers**
>
> 1 releases 2 surrounded 3 exploded 4 ash
> 5 erupted 6 regions 7 sample 8 monitored

PREDICTING CONTENT FROM VISUALS

3 👥 Students complete the task in pairs. Encourage them to study the pictures carefully. Even if they are not sure where the photographs were taken, or what is happening in the photographs, they should try to guess.

4 ▶️👤 Students watch and check their answers.

> **Answers**
>
> The video focuses on the work of a vulcanologist (a person who studies volcanoes) in Russia.

UNDERSTANDING MAIN IDEAS

5 ▶️👤 Ask the students to read the eight words in the box and to try and remember which ones were mentioned in the video. Then play the clip a second time and ask them to complete the summary and compare their answers in pairs. Elicit the answers from the class.

> **Answers**
>
> 1 volcanic 2 California 3 vulcanologist
> 4 ash 5 samples 6 volcano

WHILE WATCHING

UNDERSTANDING DETAIL

6 ▶️👤 Ask the students to read the sentences and to decide from memory whether they are true or false. Play the clip again and ask the students to check their answers. Quickly go through the answers with the class. With a stronger group, you could ask the students to rewrite the false sentences to make them correct (or to correct them orally).

> **Answers**
>
> 1 T 2 T 3 T 4 F 5 T 6 T 7 T 8 F

DISCUSSION

7 👥👥 Give the students 2–3 minutes to discuss the questions. You could also ask the groups to discuss any volcanoes they know of that have erupted, either recently or well-known historic eruptions. Elicit some ideas for each question from some of the groups.

LISTENING 1

PRONUNCIATION FOR LISTENING

> **Optional activity**
>
> Write the following on the board and ask the students to try and say them out loud in pairs or small groups, comparing the difference between the two:
>
> /duː/ /ʌɪ/ /hæv/ /tʌɪm/ (= do I have time, with each word articulated individually)
>
> /dəwʌɪhævtʌɪm/ (= do I have time, spoken naturally with the connecting /w/ sound and weak form in the word do)
>
> Monitor the students as they practice saying the phrases out loud, giving feedback as appropriate. Note down the names of one or two students who are pronouncing the two examples well. Then call on one or more of these students to model the pronunciation of each example, and ask the class which sounds the most natural.
>
> This is worth trying even if your students are not used to working with the IPA. It is very likely that students will be able to work out the pronunciation, especially if they are working in pairs or small groups. Students often enjoy working out puzzles, codes and other challenges – and this is a good way of introducing the IPA to your students.
>
> If your students enjoy this task, you could recommend that they note down the phonetic spelling of some of the words they learn during the lesson. Good dictionaries include IPA spelling, and with a little practice, your students will find that they can learn the different sounds very quickly. This will help the students learn the correct pronunciation of new words, and will be a useful tool for students as they become more advanced language learners.

1 🔊 5.1 👤 Students complete the task individually and compare their answers in pairs. Quickly go through the answers with the class. You could ask them to repeat the sentences in their pairs, and to try and sound as natural as possible.

> **Answers**
>
> 1 /w/ 2 /r/ 3 /r/ 4 /w/

PREPARING TO LISTEN

UNDERSTANDING KEY VOCABULARY

2 Students complete the task individually or in pairs. Point out that the words in bold are especially important, and will be used in a lecture later on in the unit. Elicit the answers from the class.

> **Answers**
> 1 c 2 d 3 a 4 e 5 b 6 f 7 g

PREDICTING CONTENT FROM VISUALS

3 Give the students around two minutes to discuss the questions. Remind them to base their ideas on the vocabulary they have been working with as well as the pictures on page 91. Quickly elicit some ideas from the class, but do not comment on whether or not they are correct.

WHILE LISTENING

LISTENING FOR MAIN IDEAS

4 ◀) 5.2 Students complete the task individually. You could ask the students to read the questions and to try to guess the answers before listening to the recording. If so, the students should then check their answers against the recording. Quickly go through the answers with the class.

> **Answers**
> 1 sea water
> 2 in extreme climates
> 3 solar power
> 4 no chemicals
> 5 can help solve the global food problem

LISTENING FOR DETAIL

5 ◀) 5.3 Students complete the task individually. You could ask the students to discuss the possible answers in pairs before listening to the recording. It will be difficult for your students to guess correctly, but this will help ensure that they are well prepared for the second part of the lecture. Quickly go through the answers with the class.

> **Answers**
> 1 (only) 100 metres
> 2 sun
> 3 (sea) water
> 4 160
> 5 (up to) 10,000
> 7 environment

POST-LISTENING

LISTENING FOR TEXT ORGANIZATION FEATURES

6 Ask the students to read the information box. Students then complete the task individually.

> **Answers**
> 1 d 2 a 3 c 4 b

DISCUSSION

7 Students complete the task in small groups. Encourage them to explain their ideas fully. For example, why do they think that it is/isn't important to eat organic food? Allow up to five minutes for discussion, then elicit ideas from the class.

You could open the feedback session up as a class discussion on attitudes towards food. Do the people who live in the students' country generally have a good diet? Is it possible to generalize, or does diet change depending on the area or socio-economic group (= income and status in society)? How has diet changed over the years? Who in the class is able to cook for themselves, and what ingredients do they like to use/dishes do they like to prepare? You could also take a more global approach, and ask the class which countries they think have the best diet and which countries have the worst.

⊙ LANGUAGE DEVELOPMENT

NEGATIVE PREFIXES

> **Language note**
> You can often guess the meaning of new words if you know the meaning of their prefixes. For example, *de-* means 'remove or take away'. So, *desalination* means 'without salt' and *decaffeinated* means 'without caffeine'.

1 👤👥 Students complete the task individually and compare their answers in pairs.

Answers

prefix	examples
un-	unknown unbelievable uncertain unlimited
in-	incorrect indirect inexperienced
im-	immodest immature
ir-	irresponsible
il-	illegal
dis-	disapprove disadvantage
de-	deactivate decaffeinated defrost
mis-	misunderstand misplace misspell mistreat
anti-	anti-government anti-clockwise anti-war

2 👤 Students complete the task individually and check their answers in pairs. Quickly go through the answers with the class.

Answers

1 misspell 2 unbelievable 3 disadvantage
4 uncertain 5 illegal 6 irresponsible 7 inexperienced
8 misunderstood

MODALS TO EXPRESS OPINIONS

Language note

Modal verbs such as *can*, *might* and *must* can be used to show a level of certainty about an idea.

You could remind your students of some or all of the following aspects of modals when used to express opinions or things that are possible:

- They have no third person -*s*:

  He might go to the cinema tonight. (NOT *He mights go to the cinema tonight*).

- Questions, negatives, short answers and tags are made without *do*.

  He shouldn't be allowed to run a business. (NOT *He doesn't should be allowed to run a business.*)

- They use the infinitive without *to*:
  I **might phone** her tonight.
  I **must phone** her tonight.
  I **should phone** her tonight.
  I **could phone** her tonight.

3 👥 Ask the students to read the information box, and to discuss the difference between the two sentences in pairs.

Answers

1 is stating a fact
2 is altering the message by recognizing that this may or may not be true

4 👥 Elicit suggestions from the class.

Answers

The modal verbs *could* and *may* can be used without changing the meaning.
Using *will* would make this a certain statement.

5 🔊5.4 👤 Students complete the task individually. Quickly go through the answers with the class.

Answers

1 may
2 could
3 might

6 👥 Students complete the task in pairs. Quickly go through the answers with the class.

Answers

a 1 b 2 c 2 d 1

7 👤👥 Students complete the task individually or in pairs. Point out that more than one modal may be possible in one or more of the sentences. Elicit the answers from the class.

Possible answers

2 Not using fossil fuels **might/could/may reduce** global warming.
3 Taxing fossil fuels **will reduce** the use of cars.
4 Using solar energy **will not/cannot lead to** environmental disasters.

LISTENING 2

PREPARING TO LISTEN

UNDERSTANDING KEY VOCABULARY

> **Optional activity**
>
> 👥 Ask students to close their books. Draw a quick sketch of a wind farm on the board (use the one on page 95 as a model) and elicit the term 'wind farm' or 'wind energy' from the class. If they suggest that the drawing is a windmill, tell them that they are close – but you have drawn something that produces energy, not flour. Then put the students into small groups and ask them to discuss the following questions.
>
> - *Does your country use wind farms for energy?*
> - *What are the advantages and disadvantages of wind farms?*
> - *Would you support greater use of wind farms instead of more traditional sources of energy?*
> - *Would you be happy to have a wind farm near your home?*
>
> Give the students up to five minutes to discuss the questions, then elicit ideas form each group. You could open this up to a class discussion, or a debate.

1 👤 Ask the students to read the text and to decide which arguments they agree with most. Elicit ideas from the class. If you haven't already done the optional introduction above, you could open this up to a class discussion. If so, encourage the students to support their arguments with examples. If internet access is available, you could give them a few minutes to research the topic further online before discussing their ideas.

2 👤 Students complete the task individually and check their answers in pairs. Quickly elicit the answers from the class.

> **Answers**
>
> 2 risk 3 provides 4 long-term 5 disasters
> 6 environmentally friendly 7 source 8 affordable
> 9 opponents 10 pollute

3 👥 Give the students 3–5 minutes to discuss their ideas and take notes in small groups. Quickly elicit ideas from the class, but do not comment in too much detail at this stage.

4 🔊 5.5 👤 Students listen to the recording and compare their ideas. Quickly go through the advantages and disadvantages as discussed in the recording with the class.

WHILE LISTENING

LISTENING FOR DETAIL

5 🔊 5.5 👤 Students complete the task individually. Quickly elicit the answers from the class. With a stronger class, you could ask them to try and answer the questions from memory and then check their answers against the recording.

> **Answers**
>
> 1 a, c 2 a, b, d 3 a, d

POST-LISTENING

6 👤👥 Ask the students to read the information box and to quickly read the three extracts to find examples of the language of counter-arguments. Elicit suggestions from the class. Then ask the students to complete the task individually or in pairs.

> **Answers**
>
> 1 the idea that nuclear power is a big risk
> 2 the idea that nuclear energy does not pollute the air
> 3 the idea that solar or wind energy are greener than nuclear energy

DISCUSSION

7 👤👥 Ask the class the following question: *In this country, who would decide on whether or not to build a nuclear power plant? The government? The local council? Someone else?* Elicit ideas from the class, and try to get the class to agree on who is responsible for these decisions. If no one knows, ask them to find out for the next class by using an English-language search engine. Remind them that most search engines can be set to return results in English only, and that this can be a useful way of developing their English-language skills outside of class. Then tell the class that they should imagine that they are in a country where decisions concerning the building of nuclear power plants are left to local councils, rather than national government. Stage the task as follows.

Tell the students to take out a piece of paper and a pen, and to work alone. Tell them to write down either 'I am for nuclear power' or 'I am against nuclear power' on the paper. They should not discuss this with anyone else at this stage.

Give them two minutes to make notes individually on why they are for/against.

Put the students in to groups of 4–5. Appoint one person to chair the meeting and a secretary to minute the meeting (= take notes). The chair and secretary can also contribute to the meeting. Try to make sure that you have a good balance of male and female chairs and secretaries across all groups. Students discuss their ideas in their groups.

When everyone has spoken and discussed each other's ideas, the chair should get the group to reach a decision on which the whole groups can agree. When a decision has been reached, the chair should summarize the decision to make sure that everyone is clear on what has been decided. Once agreed, the secretary should note down the decision taken.

The secretaries then present the decision taken to the class.

CRITICAL THINKING

UNDERSTAND

Background note

Farmers, scientists, politicians and other stakeholders have debated a number of ways of how to feed a growing world population in a changing climate. Experts say that food production will have to increase by at least 60% by 2050 to feed a world population of (by then) over 9 billion.

Genetically modified (GM) crops are one possible solution. Other ideas include using drought-protecting chemicals to protect crops from high temperatures, printing food (artificial meat and chocolate have already been produced this way), using synthetic biology to produce life from scratch, using 'forgotten' grains and other foods from hundreds of years ago that are more tolerant to poor conditions, and finding ways to encourage the human race to evolve to be smaller.

Since the dawn of agriculture, farmers have used cross-breeding techniques to grow stronger, healthier crops. This process is very slow, and it can take years to reach the desired goal. GM techniques can be used to achieve the same goal far more quickly. Rather then cross-breeding different strains of crops, scientists take a desirable gene from one plant and insert it into another. This technology has proven very controversial and many governments have banned the sale of GM food for human consumption. This is true of the UK, although meat from animals reared on GM crops is widely available. In the US, GM food has been available for human consumption for years, although must be clearly labelled.

It is important for your students to understand that GM crops and organic crops are not opposites as such. Organic crops can be most helpfully compared to crops grown using pesticides. It is possible to buy meat from animals that have not been fed GM food, but which is not organic because these animals were reared on crops grown using chemical pesticides. Likewise, the majority of non-GM food destined for human consumption is not organic, as it has been grown using such pesticides.

This is an area which can arouse passionate, but often ill-informed, debate. If there is time available, it would be worth encouraging your students to research the topic in English either before they debate the subject (to make their arguments more informed) or after they discuss the issues covered in this section (to see whether anything they read makes them change their mind on the topic).

1 👥 👥 Students complete the task in pairs or groups of three. Tell them to pay special attention when answering questions 2 and 3, which may not be as straightforward as they first seem (see background notes above). Allow three minutes for discussion, then elicit ideas from the students. Make sure that by the end of the discussion, the students are clear on the answers to questions 1 and 2. They may need to further research question 3, as this will depend on local laws. However, note that some countries ban the sale of GM food to humans but not for animal feed, so it may be that the meat available in the shops has been reared on GM food.

Answers

1 food which comes from an organism that has been altered by scientists in a laboratory
2 Organic food comes from plants which have grown naturally without chemicals or any other artificial treatment.

APPLY

2 👥 👥 Students complete the task in pairs or groups of three. In countries which ban the sale of GM food for human consumption, there is no need to do question 3. In such countries, you could modify question 3 to *Would you mind eating food that has been genetically modified? Why/Why not?* Allow up to two minutes for discussion, then quickly elicit some ideas from the class.

ANALYZE

3 Students complete the task individually and check their answers in pairs. Quickly elicit answers from the students.

> **Answers**
>
> 1 positive 2 negative 3 negative 4 positive

CREATE

4 Students complete the task individually. It would be useful if the students could spend some time researching this topic online before deciding whether or not they agree with the arguments, or what possible counter-arguments there might be.

EVALUATE

5 Students complete the task in small groups. Allow 5–15 minutes for the discussion, depending on the level of preparation and research that the students have done. If the students are basing their ideas on their own gut feelings, five minutes should be enough.

SPEAKING

PREPARATION FOR SPEAKING

LINKING IDEAS

1 Tell students that this task focuses on words and phrases used to link ideas. Ask them to quickly read the words/phrases in the box for examples. Then give the students up to five minutes to complete the task. When the students are ready, ask them to quickly complete or check their answers with a partner.

> **Answers**
>
> 2 However 3 First of all 4 Secondly 5 overall
> 6 comparison 7 well as that 8 the other hand

2 Students complete the task individually and check their answers in pairs. Do not go through the answers at this stage; ask the students to go on to Exercise 3.

3 Students complete the task individually and check their answers in pairs.

> **Answers**
>
> | explaining a sequence of ideas | comparing and contrasting ideas | adding another idea | summarizing ideas |
> |---|---|---|---|
> | To begin with First of all Secondly Next Finally Firstly | However On the other hand In comparison Despite that In contrast Although but | As well as … Also What's more And In addition | Overall All in all To sum up |

4 Students complete the task individually and check their answers in pairs.

> **Answers**
>
> 1 Also 2 Firstly; What's more 3 In addition
> 4 Despite that 5 To sum up

TALKING ABOUT ADVANTAGES AND DISADVANTAGES

5 Students complete the task individually and check their answers in pairs.

> **Answers**
>
> 1 advantages 2 disadvantages 3 advantages
> 4 advantages 5 disadvantages 6 disadvantages

6 Give the students 3–5 minutes to complete the task individually. Monitor the class as they write their sentences down, giving feedback as appropriate.

7 Students complete the task individually and check their answers in pairs. Allow up to two minutes for discussion, then quickly elicit one answer for each question from the class.

SPEAKING TASK

PREPARE

1 Tell the students that following the town council's decision to build a nuclear power plant, the town has been granted city status and an increased budget. The members of the newly formed city council must now decide how to use the extra money. Ask them to read

the notes in the box and then to get in to groups of four and decide on their roles.

2 👥 Tell the students to make sure that they have read, understood and internalized their roles. Their job is to really become that person during the next speaking task. Give them up to three minutes to make notes based on how they think that their character would act.

PRACTISE

3 👥 Students complete the task in groups of three. Make sure that they are now working only with students who will be playing the same role. If it is not possible to have groups of three, one or more groups can be slightly larger. Tell them to discuss the advantages and disadvantages from their own perspective, but also to try and anticipate what the other characters will say. You could give them some more time to consider the other characters' possible views in more depth, in which case they could first quickly read the other role cards to find out more about the other roles. Allow up to 10 minutes for the groups to prepare this task in depth, ready for Exercise 5.

4 👥 Encourage the students to assess their performance objectively, and to invite and give constructive criticism from the other group members.

DISCUSS

5 👥 Put students in to groups of four, each student with a different character. Appoint one person to chair the meeting and a secretary to minute the meeting (= take notes). The chair and secretary can also contribute to the meeting. Try to make sure that you have a good balance of male and female chairs and secretaries across all groups. Monitor the groups and take notes for later class feedback. Try not to intervene in the group discussions unless you hear a very basic error that needs to be corrected immediately. Tell the students that they have up to 10 minutes for group discussion, by which time they must reach a decision for the secretary to present to the class. Give them a two-minute warning before the 10 minutes are up.

6 The secretaries then present the decision taken to the class.

TASK CHECKLIST AND OBJECTIVES REVIEW

Refer students to the end of each unit for the Task checklist and Objectives review. Students complete the tables individually to reflect on their learning and identify areas for improvement.

WORDLIST

See Teaching tips, pages 9–11 for ideas about how to make the most of the Wordlist with your students.

REVIEW TEST

See pages 106–107 for the photocopiable Review test for this unit, and page 91 for ideas about when and how to administer the Review test.

ADDITIONAL SPEAKING TASK

See page 122 for an Additional speaking task related to this unit.

Put students in small groups and focus them on the discussion topic. Give them up to three minutes to make notes on the ideas before giving them the chance to discuss them. Allow up to 10 minutes for the interaction, and then ask each group to report back to the whole class.

RESEARCH PROJECT

Create an advert to sell 'green' energy sources.

Divide the class and ask them to think about alternative, 'green' sources of energy. Examples could be solar, tidal, geothermic, wind, hydroelectric and biomass. Give each group one of these to research in depth. Ask students to think about how that way of sourcing energy works, its advantages, and compare it to the process of getting energy from fossil fuels such as oil, gas and coal.

Ask each group to produce a video to advertise their way of sourcing 'green' energy, using media of their choice, in order to 'sell' it to people. Videos can be uploaded to a video-sharing website.

HEALTH AND FITNESS

Learning objectives

Before you start the *Unlock your knowledge* section, ask students to read the Learning objectives box. This will give them a clear idea of what they will learn in the unit. Tell them that you will return to these objectives at the end of the unit, when they review what they have learned. Give students the opportunity to ask any questions they might have.

UNLOCK YOUR KNOWLEDGE

Background note

The photo shows people doing T'ai chi in Shanghai. T'ai chi is a Chinese martial art which is said to have many health benefits. People perform a series of slow movements which help their posture and breathing.

Optional lead in

Write the word *diet* on the board and elicit its meaning(s) from the class. The word has three distinct meanings, the first two of which are related to food. Students do not need to know the third meaning for the purposes of this unit.

1 the food and drink usually eaten or drunk by a person or group: *Diet varies between different countries in the world.*

2 an eating plan in which someone eats less food, or only particular types of food, because they want to become thinner or for medical reasons: *The doctor put me on a low-salt diet to reduce my blood pressure.*

3 a particular type of thing that you experience or do regularly, or a limited range of activities: *The TV only offers a diet of comedies and old movies every evening.*

Elicit from the class whether people in their country have, generally speaking, a healthy diet. Encourage discussion where there is disagreement. At this stage, keep the discussion fairly general. Students will have the opportunity to discuss their own attitude towards diet and fitness later. You could also ask them what can happen when people have a poor diet.

👥 Give the students 2–3 minutes to discuss the questions in pairs, then elicit ideas from the class. You could also ask whether the students think that it would really be desirable to live to be 100 years old.

WATCH AND LISTEN

▶ Video script

Rian Gonzales is a 39-year-old computer programmer from California. He is overweight.

To help lose weight he has run six marathons. His goal is now to participate in the Malibu triathlon. A triathlon is a fitness event where participants swim, cycle and run. The Malibu triathlon consists of: an 800-metre swim, a 30-kilometre bike ride and a six and a half kilometre run.

The hardest part of the triathlon for Rian will be the swim. He is afraid of the water because he almost drowned as a child.

He hires a swimming coach to help him train. Soon he can swim twice as far as he was able to a week ago. To help in the cycling section of the triathlon, Rian goes to a specialist shop and gets some professional cycling clothes and shoes to wear. Rian is given a bike to ride made of carbon fibre and aluminium, which is very light. He goes out cycling and soon feels a lot more comfortable on the bicycle.

A week before the triathlon, Rian collects his wetsuit. This will keep him warm when he does the triathlon sea swim. He puts on the wetsuit and goes training with a friend. He swims 400 metres in the ocean, half the distance he needs to swim in the competition. He is almost ready to take part in the triathlon.

The day of the triathlon arrives. Rian is nervous but he gets ready to enter the water. The triathlon starts and he begins the swim. He gets out of the water and starts the cycling part of the race. The bike ride is tough.

Rian runs the third part of the triathlon. Finally, he finishes the race. His friends meet him at the end. Rian has now accomplished the goal of finishing his first triathlon, and hopes to do many more in the future.

PREPARING TO WATCH

UNDERSTANDING KEY VOCABULARY

1 👤 Students complete the task individually and check their answers in pairs. Quickly elicit the answers from the students.

| Answers |
| 1 c 2 f 3 d 4 e 5 b 6 a |

USING YOUR KNOWLEDGE TO PREDICT CONTENT

2 👥 Give the students 1–2 minutes to discuss the task in pairs, then elicit ideas from the class. Encourage the students to support their ideas with evidence from the photos.

3 ▶ Students watch and check their answers in pairs.

> **Answers**
> 1 b   2 a   3 c   4 a

WHILE WATCHING

UNDERSTANDING MAIN IDEAS

4 ▶👤 Students complete the task individually and compare their answers in pairs. With stronger groups, you could ask them first to try to complete the summary from memory before watching the video again to check and complete their answers. Quickly elicit the answers from the class.

> **Answers**
> 1 lose weight   2 triathlon   3 swim   4 drowned
> 5 clothes   6 shoes   7 light   8 wetsuit   9 sea   10 swim
> 11 bike (bicycle)   12 runs

UNDERSTANDING DETAIL

5 ▶👤 Students complete the task individually and compare their answers in pairs. Again, with stronger groups, you could ask them first to try to answer the questions from memory before watching the video again to check and complete their answers. Quickly elicit the answers from the class.

> **Answers**
> 1 F   2 DNS   3 F   4 T   5 F   6 T   7 DNS   8 F   9 T   10 DNS

DISCUSSION

6 👥 Students complete the task in small groups. For question 1, you could also ask the students whether they would be interested in entering at least one of the triathlon events (running, cycling or swimming).

LISTENING 1

PREPARING TO LISTEN

UNDERSTANDING KEY VOCABULARY

1 👤 Students complete the task individually and check their answers in pairs. Quickly elicit the answers from the students.

> **Answers**
> 1 b   2 e   3 c   4 g   5 d   6 a   7 f

USING YOUR KNOWLEDGE

2 👥 Give the students 2–4 minutes to discuss the questions in small groups. You could also ask them to discuss which photograph best represents their own lifestyle. Quickly elicit ideas from the class. Although it is clear that both lifestyle and genes affect health to some extent, there is no need to encourage the students to come to this conclusion at this stage (although they may well do so anyway). More information will be provided in the listening task.

WHILE LISTENING

LISTENING FOR MAIN IDEAS

3 🔊 6.1 👤 Students complete the task individually. You could ask the students to discuss the possible answers before listening to the recording. Quickly go through the answers with the class.

> **Answers**
> 1 Not always – some older people may have smoked or never exercised regularly.
> 2 Genes may be more important than lifestyle when it comes to a long life.

> **Optional activity**
>
> 👥 Ask students to read the information box and to discuss what kinds of clues can help us decide what a speaker is thinking or feeling. Allow a few minutes for discussion, then elicit ideas from the class.
>
> (Possible answers include: the language people use, intonation, body language and whether or not the speaker maintains eye contact. Note that to a certain extent, all of these suggestions may be culturally specific. You could ask your students to discuss ways that people in their culture show agreement and disagreement, and then ask them to contrast this with another culture that they know about.)

LISTENING FOR ATTITUDE

4 👥 Give the students up to two minutes to discuss the statement in pairs. Remind them that they must give reasons for their opinions. You could also do this task as a group activity.

5 🔊 **6.2** 👥 Ask students to read the opinions and to decide in pairs whether or not the speakers agree with the statement in Exercise 4. Play the recording. Give students the opportunity to change their answers, then elicit the answers from the class.

> **Answers**
>
> Speaker A: agrees
> Speaker B: agrees
> Speaker C: disagrees
> Speaker D: disagrees

PRONUNCIATION FOR LISTENING

6 🔊 **6.3** 👤👥 Ask the students to read the information and then to read the five sentences. Before playing the recording, ask the students to decide individually or in pairs how each speaker feels. Give them 1–2 minutes to decide, then tell the students that they are going to hear each speaker say their sentences. Tell students to play close attention to the intonation and to check their answers. Do they still agree with their first thoughts? Quickly go through the answers with the class. You could then play the recording again, stopping after each speaker and asking the class how they would describe the speaker's intonation (e.g. uncertain, positive, cynical, etc.).

> **Answers**
>
> 1 positive/enthusiastic (wide pitch range, emphasis on *great*)
> 2 certain (emphatic stress on *no question* and *happy people live longer*)
> 3 certain, and against getting worried (stress on *ridiculous*)
> 4 cynical (doesn't have wide pitch range in first sentence; question ends on falling tone, which indicates that the speaker isn't really seeking an answer)
> 5 uncertain (flat pitch range throughout, doesn't stress *great*, but stresses *but*)

POST-LISTENING

> **Language note**
>
> As the explanation box says, phrases such as *Everyone knows that* and *Most people think that* are often used by speakers or writers who wish to make their arguments stronger. However, such phrases can be misused. Speakers sometimes use such phrases when they want to make their own opinions sound more authoritative. It is often impossible to really know what 'most people' think, unless the speaker has access to extensive data from, for example, opinion polls (which can still give a very inaccurate picture of a population's opinions).
>
> When misused, these kinds of phrases are often referred to as *weasel words* – words that someone says either to avoid answering a question clearly or to make someone believe something that is not true (or which cannot be proven).
>
> Students should be very careful when using these kinds of phrases, especially when it comes to presenting arguments during debates or writing academic essays and papers. Wherever possible, students should refer to research and evidence to support their arguments. Simply claiming that 'everyone knows' something may give the impression that the student has based his or her arguments on their own subjective understanding of a topic rather than objective research. If these phrases are to be used, it is better for students to use them only when discussing objective fact rather than subjective opinion.

7 👥 Students complete the task in pairs. Give them 2–4 minutes to discuss the extent to which they agree with the statements. In each case, the student should say why they agree/disagree. Quickly elicit some ideas from the class. You could ask the students to research one or more of the claims as an internet homework task. If so, you could ask them to prepare a very short talk on their findings for the next class.

8 👤 Give the students 3–5 minutes to complete the task individually. Monitor the students as they write, giving feedback as appropriate.

9 👥 Students discuss their ideas in small groups. Encourage the students to question each other's statements. How can they be certain? Are the claims they are making objective fact or subjective opinion? What research could be done to make their claims more reliable? Give the students 5–10 minutes to discuss their ideas, then elicit examples from the class. Encourage class discussion, especially whenever a potentially contentious statement (a statement that other people might disagree with) is made.

👁 LANGUAGE DEVELOPMENT

PHRASAL VERBS

Language note
A phrasal verb is a phrase that consists of a verb with a particle (a preposition or adverb or both), the meaning of which is different from the meaning of its separate parts. *Look after, work out* and *make up for* are all examples of phrasal verbs.
Sometimes the meaning can be understood by looking at both (in some cases, all) parts of a phrasal verb. However, sometimes the meaning is not obvious. This is especially true of phrasal verbs that have more than one meaning, such as *work out*.
1 to happen or develop in a particular way: *Let's hope this new job **works out** well for him.*
2 to exercise in order to improve the strength or appearance of your body: *Huw **works out** in the gym two or three times a week.*
3 to be the result of a calculation: *In fact the trip **worked out** cheaper than we'd expected.*

1 👤 Ask students to read the explanation box and to complete the exercise individually. Quickly elicit the answers from the students.

> **Answers**
>
> 2 brought up 3 take up 4 take over 5 give up

2 👤 Students complete the task individually and check their answers in pairs. The first one has been done for them as an example. Quickly elicit the answers from the students.

> **Answers**
>
> b give up c take up d bring up e take over

3 🔊 6.4 👤 Students complete the task individually and check their answers in pairs. With a stronger class, you could ask them to try and complete the task in pairs before listening to the recording. Quickly elicit the answers from the students.

> **Answers**
>
> 1 on 2 over 3 up 4 down 5 on 6 out

4 👤 Students complete the task individually and check their answers in pairs. Quickly elicit the answers from the students.

> **Answers**
>
> a break down b went on c get on (with)
> d make out e get over f sign up (for)

5 👥 Give the students up to 10 minutes to complete the task in pairs. Ask them to take it in turns to answer each question, and to ask each other further questions based on their answers. This is a personal task, and could generate a lot of useful discussion, so allow it to run for as long as the students seem engaged. Monitor the students during the discussion and take notes on their use of language (both correct and incorrect). When the students have finished their discussions, give some examples of some of the especially good language that you heard. Pick out some of the typical errors that students are making (in grammar, vocabulary and pronunciation) and elicit corrections from the class where possible.

TALKING ABOUT PREFERENCES

6 👤 Students complete the task individually and check their answers in pairs. Quickly elicit the answers from the students.

> **Answers**
>
> 1 no
> 2 the new sushi place
> 3 no
> 4 stay at home and study

7 👥 Students complete the task in pairs. Ask them to read the role cards and to begin as soon as they are ready. Monitor the class and take notes for later classroom feedback.

LISTENING 2

PREPARING TO LISTEN

UNDERSTANDING KEY VOCABULARY

1 👤 Students complete the task individually and compare their answers in pairs. Quickly go through the answers with the class.

> **Answers**
>
> 1 a 2 e 3 f 4 g 5 b 6 c 7 d

USING YOUR KNOWLEDGE

2 👥 Students complete the task in pairs. Ask them, to briefly discuss what they know about each of the treatments. Elicit the answers from the class, and ask the students what they can tell you about each treatment. Do not comment in detail at this stage, as more information will be given in the next listening exercise.

> **Answers**
>
> 1 B 2 D 3 C 4 A

WHILE LISTENING

LISTENING FOR MAIN IDEAS

3 🔊 6.5 👤 Students complete the task individually and check their answers in pairs. Quickly elicit the answers from the students.

> **Answers**
>
> 1 meditation 2 aloe vera 3 aromatherapy
> 4 acupuncture

LISTENING FOR DETAIL

4 🔊 6.5 👤👥 Students complete the task individually or in pairs. Quickly elicit the answers from the class. With a stronger class, you could ask them to try and complete the task in pairs before listening to the recording a second time to check their answers.

> **Answers**
>
> | | meditation | aloe vera | aromatherapy | acupuncture |
> |---|---|---|---|---|
> | poor concentration | ✓ | | | |
> | stress | ✓ | | ✓ | |
> | sleep problems | | | ✓ | |
> | being overweight | | | | ✓ |
> | skin problems | | ✓ | ✓ | |
> | stomach problems | | ✓ | | |

DISCUSSION

5 👥 Give the students up to five minutes to discuss the questions in small groups. Tell the students to support their answer to question

4 with examples if possible. You could give them some time to research question 4. If so, encourage the class to look at authoritative websites that give objective facts rather than discussion forums which are open to anyone, and which are often unedited and unmoderated. As a follow up to question 4, you could ask the students if they can think of examples as to when alternative therapies might actually be harmful (e.g. a homoeopathist could diagnose sugar pills as a way of treating a serious condition, when it would actually be in the patient's best interests to seek the advice of a qualified doctor).

6 👥👥 Students complete the task and discuss their ideas in pairs or small groups.

> **Answers**
>
> Adjectives: new, free, best, fresh, natural, delicious, full, clean, wonderful, special, big, bright
> Verbs: make, get, see, love, come, feel

CRITICAL THINKING

UNDERSTAND

1 👥👥 Students complete the task in pairs or small groups. For the first question, you could ask the students to close their eyes as you read the advertisement aloud. They should then discuss the images and ideas that come to mind with a partner/in their groups. Invite brief feedback from two or three groups.

> **Optional activity**
>
> 👥 Students choose their least favourite of the two advertisements and redraft it to make it more appealing. Tell the class that they will present their advertisements in five minutes, after which the class will clap according to how much they enjoyed the advertisement. The group with the loudest/longest clap wins. The teacher plays the role of 'clapometer' to judge the winning group. Tell students to keep their advertisements simple, as they will get the opportunity to write a more detailed advertisement in the next task.

2 👥 Students decide on the two products with a partner.

3 👤 Students complete the exercise individually.

4 👥 Students complete the task in pairs. Encourage them to support their ideas with examples from their own experience of successful advertisements. Give the students 2–3 minutes to discuss their ideas, then quickly elicit some suggestions from the class.

APPLY

5 👥👥👥 Students complete the task in small groups (there should be an even number of groups). This is best done as a discussion task, with *two* people in each group taking detailed notes for use during Exercise 6. Allow five minutes for discussion.

CREATE

6 👥👥👥 Students complete the task in small groups. They do not need to complete the advertising campaign, but they should have an overall concept by the end of their discussions. Emphasize to the class that they are discussing an advertising campaign, not just one possible advert. An advertising campaign would usually involve the use of mixed media (internet, TV, radio, podcasts, cinema, posters, newspapers and magazines, etc.).

7 👥👥👥 One of the students who took notes during Exercise 5 from each group should swap places with a student from another group. That student presents their group's ideas and invites questions, suggestions and observations. The new group then do the same with their ideas. Allow 5–10 minutes for discussion, then ask the students who swapped places to go back to their original groups. Those students should then give details of the other group's ideas to their own group.

Optional activity

👥👥👥 Students plan a detailed advertising campaign based on their earlier discussions. In class, the students should decide what kind of media they would like to use, which magazines/websites, etc. they should target (and why) and who will be responsible for which part of the campaign. They then divide up the work and prepare their campaign as a homework task. For example, two students could write a radio script for a 30-second 'spot', one could design a poster, another could design a newspaper advertisement, etc. Encourage the students to play to their strengths, so a student with good design skills should be responsible for the poster, students interested in drama could script a TV advertisement, etc. Tell the students to be ready to present their ideas during the next class. In the following class, the students present their ideas to their groups for feedback, make any amendments necessary and then present each section of the campaign to the rest of the class. Any sections of the campaign than involve acting should be acted out for the class, with a follow-up commentary being given by the student(s) responsible for that section of the campaign.

If you have computers or tablets available in the class, this could also be done during class time.

SPEAKING

PREPARATION FOR SPEAKING

PROBLEM–SOLUTION ORGANIZATION

1 👥👥 Students complete the task in pairs. Allow plenty of time for discussion, then elicit the answers from the class.

Answers

1 to engage the audience and make them think about the topic
2 to make them think about their own problems – these are all yes/no questions, and it is likely that many people would answer 'yes' to some of them. This sets up the advert as a solution to the audience's problems.
3 feeling tired, feeling stressed, problems concentrating
4 meditation
5 to try and make it 'common knowledge' that everyone knows that meditation is helpful
6 yes, to increase energy and happiness levels
7 the name of the place offering classes, the price of an introductory class, and the time.
8 an imperative verb form – it's used to give a suggestion or an instruction to the audience

2 👤👥👥 Students complete the task individually or in pairs. Quickly elicit the answers from the class.

Answers

specific information about the place, time, etc. 4
background information about the treatment 3
rhetorical questions to attract the listeners' attention 1
introduction of the treatment 2

USING IMPERATIVES TO PERSUADE

Language note

Persuasive language can be used for a number of purposes. In this unit, we have seen such language used in advertisements to encourage consumers to believe that they need or want a particular product. Earlier in the unit, we saw examples of how persuasive language can be used to help forward a convincing argument. Examples of this kind of language can also be found in political propaganda, public speaking and academic writing.

The kind of persuasive language we use will depend on its purpose. Imperatives are generally not appropriate in academic discourse as they tend to encourage subjectivity. However, they are extremely useful in advertising. This is because imperatives encourage the potential customer to do something quickly; imperatives can also make people feel that they have no other choice but to buy the product or service advertised.

In sentences like *Buy now!*, *Call today!*, and *Visit our website!*, the verb forms *buy, call* and *visit* are called imperatives. Positive imperatives have the same form as the bare infinitive (the infinitive without *to*). Negative imperatives are constructed with *do not/don't* (e.g. *Don't delay!*).

Note that we don't use a subject with imperative sentences. For example, we say *Buy now!* not ~~You buy now!~~

It is interesting to note that this form of the verb is also used for giving orders, and that the word *imperative* means 'important or urgent'. This sense of importance or urgency can be used very successfully by advertisers.

As well as being used to give orders or to persuade, imperatives are also used to give advice or instructions, to make offers and suggestions, and to express good wishes towards people (e.g. *Have a nice day!*).

3 Students complete the task individually or in pairs. Quickly elicit the answers from the class.

> **Answers**
>
> 2 Visit 3 Imagine 4 Call; Let 5 join 6 Learn

4 Students complete the task in pairs. Allow two minutes for discussion, then elicit the answers from the class. You could also ask the class for examples of other times that the imperative is used.

> **Answers**
>
> 1 Imperatives are often used to give commands or instructions. They can also be used to give suggestions or invitations to do something. In adverts, they can give the impression that the advert is talking directly to the listener.
> 2 Adverts want people to act. Imperative forms are used when you want someone to take action (i.e. to buy something). Imperatives do not offer the listener a choice (compared with *please could you …?*). Also, imperatives are not used to give information (compared with *Did you know that …? Or We'd like you to …*).

5 Students complete the task individually or in pairs. Quickly elicit the answers from the class.

> **Answers**
>
> 1 Buy our new product.
> 2 Buy one, get one free.
> 3 Hurry and book (a ticket) now.
> 4 Don't forget that our shops are open during the holidays.
> 5 Join our courses before it's too late!

Optional activity

A useful language-awareness task is to get your students to find examples of the use of imperatives in authentic advertisements, and to consider how effective they are. Students can then rewrite a more 'honest' version of the advertisement without using any imperatives and compare the effectiveness of this against the original.

This can be done as a homework assignment. If internet access is available in class, you could also do this during class time. This would give you the opportunity to discuss the language used in advertisements in more detail with your students, as well as giving you an interesting insight into their interests as illustrated by the advertisements they decide to look at. This can then help inform your choice of tasks and extra materials in future lessons.

USING ADJECTIVES

6 Students complete the task individually. Quickly elicit the answers from the class.

> **Answers**
>
> 1 natural; whole 2 simple; effective 3 healthy
> 4 warm; fresh 5 great; easy

7 Elicit the answer to question 1 from the class. Students discuss question 2 in pairs, then elicit suggestions. Give the students two minutes to write down as many adjectives that are typical of advertisements in pairs. Your students may not have seen many English-language advertisements, so you can ask them to write down the kinds of adjectives that would most likely be found in advertisements. Ask one pair to read their list out loud, and write the words on the board. Then go around the class adding to the list. Examples of some of the most common adjectives used in advertising are given in the answer key.

> **Answers**
>
> 1 positive
> 2 students' own answers
> 3 You could tell the class that *new, better, best, free, delicious, full, sure, clean, wonderful, special, fine, real, bright, extra, safe,* and *rich* are among the top 20 most used adjectives in advertising.

SPEAKING TASK

PREPARE

1 Students complete the task in pairs. Allow 2–3 minutes for discussion, then quickly elicit ideas from the class.

2 👥 Give the students a minute to decide on their product in pairs.

3 👥 Give the students two minutes to decide on the appropriate images and adjectives. Try to keep the pace fairly quick; as soon as you see that students are running out of ideas, you should begin eliciting suggestions from the class.

4 👥 Give students 10–15 minutes to complete the task in pairs. This is quite a demanding task, encourage the students to think carefully about each of the four points and how they should be approached in their adverts. You could point out that many people are extremely cynical about these kinds of therapies, so they will need to work hard to win these people over. Ask the class to have their adverts ready for discussion by the end of the task. Should any groups finish early, you could give them a selection of advertisements or similar products to compare against their own ideas. Alternatively, they could find examples of such adverts online.

PRACTISE

5 👥 Give the students five minutes to complete the task together with another pair. Tell the students that they will have the opportunity to make some changes to their adverts following feedback from the other pair. When each pair has presented their advert, give the students a few minutes to make any changes.

PRESENT

6 👥 Students complete the task in small groups. If at least one person in every two groups has a smartphone, that person can use their phone to record the presentation. As a follow-up task, the students who made the recordings should edit them and email the final video to you ready for you to play during the next class. Most modern smartphones have simple editing software built in to their operating systems.

Finish off by eliciting comments from the class on the adverts they heard. Were there any particularly persuasive adverts? Did any adverts succeed in changing their mind about a particular product? This stage can either be carried out following the initial group work, or following your showing of the edited videos.

TASK CHECKLIST AND OBJECTIVES REVIEW

Refer students to the end of each unit for the Task checklist and Objectives review. Students complete the tables individually to reflect on their learning and identify areas for improvement.

WORDLIST

See Teaching tips, pages 9–11 for ideas about how to make the most of the Wordlist with your students.

REVIEW TEST

See pages 108–109 for the photocopiable Review test for this unit, and page 91 for ideas about when and how to administer the Review test.

ADDITIONAL SPEAKING TASK

See page 123 for an Additional speaking task related to this unit.

Put students in groups of three. Focus them on the topic and explain that they are going to prepare a presentation for a new fitness programme.

Give them up to 10 minutes to plan their presentation, illustrating a typical week under their fitness programme. Encourage students to include details about food and exercise. Then ask students to give their presentation. Ask other groups listening to think of a question to ask after each presentation.

RESEARCH PROJECT

Create an interactive menu.

Ask students to brainstorm healthy and unhealthy foods. In groups, students can then think about two menus. One should be a choice of unhealthy foods and the other should be healthy. Each group could write a blog entry on the Cambridge LMS to share their menus with the rest of the class.

The menus can be used to create a class website (search for 'create free website'). Students can upload pictures, video and audio clips to add information about each menu item, e.g. calories, fat and alternative choices. This website can be promoted around the learning environment.

7 DISCOVERY AND INVENTION

UNLOCK YOUR KNOWLEDGE

Background note

The photos shows Difference Engine No. 2, a very early computer created by Charles Babbage in 1849. It weighed around 15 tonnes, and was 2.5 metres tall. It was able to perform a complex series of calculations automatically.

👥 👥👥 Ask the students to take out a piece of paper. Tell them that you are going to ask them a question, and they must write down the first word that comes to mind. Then ask them question 4: *What do you think is the most important invention or discovery in the last 20 years?* Very quickly elicit the answer written down by each student, then ask them to discuss the other questions in pairs or small groups.

Answers

1 The photograph shows a computer invented in 1849 by Charles Babbage.
2 An expression that means that if you really need to do something, you will think of a way of doing it. If taken more literally, it means that a particular thing is invented because there is a need for it.
3 Students' own answers.
4 Students' own answers. Encourage them to discuss their reasons for the answers in detail.

WATCH AND LISTEN

▶ Video script

Dubai: famous for its business, modern architecture, great beaches, and shopping centres. The owners of a shopping centre had a dream: to build the best indoor ski resort in the world.

Before then, the only way to ski was on the sand, called sandskiing … or use boards and 'sandboard'!

Building an indoor ski resort was an ambitious plan in a country where the temperature is regularly over 30 degrees centigrade. Ski Dubai has real snow and the world's longest indoor slope. It is built over a shopping centre.

The huge shopping centre is almost 300,000 square metres in size, and has two luxury hotels with 900 rooms, a 14-screen cinema, car parking for 7,000 cars and, of course, the ski resort.

To build Ski Dubai, engineers had to construct some of the ski slopes on the ground, and then move them up to the top of the building.

They started by lifting a 90-metre section of slope 60 metres into the air and fixing it in place.

The section weighs the same as 20 jumbo jets. It took two days to lift and position it in the correct place.

The lift started, but suddenly there was a problem. The computer system crashed and the slope was stuck in the air. However, an hour later the computer was fixed and work continued. Finally, the job was completed and the engineers celebrated the achievement.

However, on innovative projects like this there are always problems. The engineers found that there were problems with the cooling pipes. The welding work was bad and had to be replaced.

The engineers also decided to replace all the rubber pipes under the ski slope. They should not have had metal connectors because if the cooling liquid leaked out, it could have melted the 6,000 tonnes of snow at Ski Dubai. This meant that they had to dig all the pipes out of the concrete, causing a major delay to the project.

Meanwhile, a French company completed the chair lifts which take skiers to the top of the slope. After three months of hard work, Ski Dubai was finally ready and the engineers filled it with snow. It may be 30 degrees outside, but the world's first ski resort in the desert opened successfully.

PREPARING TO WATCH

UNDERSTANDING KEY VOCABULARY

1 👤 Students complete the task individually and check their answers in pairs. Quickly elicit the answers from the students.

Answers

1 c 2 d 3 e 4 b 5 a 6 f 7 h 8 j 9 i 10 g

USING VISUALS TO PREDICT CONTENT

2 Give the students two minutes to discuss the questions in pairs, then elicit ideas from the class. Encourage the students to support their ideas with evidence from the photos. As a follow-up question, you could ask students if it is actually desirable to ski in a hot country. If they are from a hot country, ask them whether there is anywhere that they can ski, or whether they would like to be able to ski in their country.

WHILE WATCHING

UNDERSTANDING MAIN IDEAS

3 Students complete the task individually and compare their answers in pairs. Again, with stronger groups, you could ask them first to try to answer the questions from memory before watching the video again to check and complete their answers. Quickly elicit the answers from the class.

4 Students complete the task individually and check their answers in pairs. To make sure that they have read and understood the questions, you could ask them to try and guess the answers in pairs before watching the video. Quickly elicit the answers from the class.

> **Answers**
>
> 1 shopping mall 2 over 3 in the air
> 4 computer crashed 5 pipes 6 French

UNDERSTANDING DETAIL

5 Students complete the task individually and compare their answers in pairs. With stronger groups, you could ask them first to try to match the numbers from memory before watching the video again to check and complete their answers. Quickly elicit the answers from the class.

> **Answers**
>
> a size of the shopping mall
> b hotels
> c rooms
> d parking spaces
> e up in the air
> f jumbo jets
> g temperature outside

DISCUSSION

6 Students discuss the questions in small groups. You could ask them to go in to some depth when answering question 3, and include references to the use of resources, the effect on the environment and the *opportunity cost* (the value of the action that you do not choose, when choosing between two possible options) of such projects. Alternatively, elicit or introduce these concepts during the post-task class feedback. Allow up to five minutes for discussion, then elicit ideas from the students.

LISTENING 1

PREPARING TO LISTEN

UNDERSTANDING KEY VOCABULARY

1 Students complete the task individually and check their answers in pairs. Quickly elicit the answers from the class.

> **Answers**
>
> 1 c 2 b 3 g 4 h 5 e 6 f 7 a 8 d

USING YOUR KNOWLEDGE

2 Give the students 2–4 minutes to discuss the questions in small groups. You could also ask them to discuss how life would be different without each of these different inventions. Elicit the answers from the class. You could also encourage some class discussion on how important each of these inventions is, and how the world would be different without any one of them

> **Answers**
>
> A gunpowder B crank shaft C chess D fountain pen

If a student asks what a *crankshaft* is, tell them that the answer will be given in the listening task (a crankshaft is a long metal rod, especially one in a car engine, that helps the engine turn the wheels).

WHILE LISTENING

LISTENING FOR MAIN IDEAS

3 🔊7.1 👤 Students complete the task individually. Quickly elicit the answers from the class.

> **Answers**
>
> 1 fountain pen 2 chess 3 crank shaft 4 gunpowder

LISTENING FOR DETAIL

4 🔊7.1 👤 Students complete the task individually and compare their answers in pairs. Again, with stronger groups, you could ask them first to try to answer the questions from memory before listening again to check and complete their answers.

> **Answers**
>
> 1 c 2 a 3 b 4 b 5 a 6 c

PRONUNCIATION FOR LISTENING

5 🔊7.2 👤 Ask the students to read the information box. Tell the students that you are going to play a recording that includes lots of weak forms, and ask them to listen carefully to the way that the words with weak forms are pronounced. Play the recording. Students complete the gaps individually and check their answers in pairs.

> **Answers**
>
> 1 from; and the; to
> 2 The; of; but the; of the; and; to; the
> 3 The; a; to; in a
> 4 of the; of

6 🔊7.3 👤 Students complete the task individually.

> **Answers**
>
> 1 b 2 c 3 a

POST-LISTENING

7 👤👥 Students complete the task individually or in pairs. Elicit the answers from the class.

> **Answers**
>
> 1 the year 953 2 the Middle Ages 3 al-Jazari
> 4 the invention of gunpowder 5 Room 14

DISCUSSION

8 👤 Give the students 3–5 minutes to complete the task individually. Monitor the students as they write, giving feedback as appropriate.

9 👥 Students discuss their ideas in small groups. Allow about two minutes' discussion time per student.

⊙ LANGUAGE DEVELOPMENT

PHRASES WITH *MAKE*

1 👤 Ask students to look at the ideas map and to complete the task individually. Ask the students to quickly check their answers in pairs. Then elicit the answers from the class.

> **Answers**
>
> 2 difference 3 mistake 4 sure 5 up my mind
> 6 friends 7 decision 8 an appointment

2 👤👥 Students complete the task individually or in pairs. The first one has been done for them as an example. Quickly elicit the answers from the students.

> **Answers**
>
> 2 force 3 cause 4 produce 5 cause 6 force

PASSIVE VERB FORMS

3 👥 Give the students 3–5 minutes to complete the task in pairs. Point out that there may be more than one possible answer.

> **Answers**
>
> 2 The Law of Gravity was discovered/developed by Isaac Newton in the 17th century.
> 3 The first computer chip was developed/invented/made/created in the 1950s.
> 4 The first smartphone was developed/invented/made/created after 1997.
> 5 Penicillin was discovered in 1928 by Alexander Fleming.

4 👤👥 Students complete the task individually or in pairs.

> **Answers**
>
> 1 was discovered 2 was invented 3 designed 4 was brought 5 was written 6 was created 7 download
> 8 are/were sent 9 was taken 10 developed

LISTENING 2

PREPARING TO LISTEN

UNDERSTANDING KEY VOCABULARY

1 👥 Students read the sentences and try to describe what an app is, or does.

> **Answers**
>
> An app is an abbreviation of *application*. It is a piece of software that you can download onto a mobile phone or a computer, which does a particular job.

2 👤 Students complete the task individually and check their answers in pairs. Point out that the first one has been given as an example, and is another form of the word *efficiently* from Exercise 1. Elicit the answers from the class.

> **Answers**
>
> 2 allows 3 leading 4 install 5 beyond
> 6 recommended 7 access 8 phenomenon 9 available

USING YOUR KNOWLEDGE TO PREDICT CONTENT

3 👥 Students discuss the questions in small groups. If possible, try to form groups that each have at least one or two students with smartphones. You could then ask those students with smartphones to talk briefly about which apps they have on their phones, and why these are so important or useful to them. Allow up to five minutes for discussion, then quickly elicit some ideas for questions 2–5 from the students. When discussing question 2, you could elicit the details of a specific app from the students.

4 🔊 7.4 👤 Students complete the task individually. You could ask them to put the topics in the most likely order before they hear the introduction, and then to check their ideas against the recording.

> **Answers**
>
> 1 c 2 a 3 b

WHILE LISTENING

LISTENING FOR MAIN IDEAS

5 👥 Students discuss their use of apps in pairs. You could ask them to discuss which ones they personally find most useful, and give one or two examples of each. You could also ask them to discuss their favourite games (if they use their smartphones to play games on).

6 🔊 7.5 👤 Students complete the task individually and check their answers in pairs.

> **Answers**
>
> mentioned: 2, 3, 4, 5, 8, 9, 11

7 🔊 7.5 👤 👥 Students complete the notes individually or in pairs. Quickly elicit the answers from the class. With a stronger class, you could ask them to try and complete the notes in pairs before listening to the recording a second time to check their answers.

> **Answers**
>
> first apps used for:
> accessing the internet
> - checking emails
> - sending texts
> second gen. apps
> - first app store opened in 2008
> - 2011 – 10 billion downloads
> - 2012 – est. 30 billion downloads
> new apps
> - more people use apps than internet browsers
> - there is a need for skilled software engineers

POST-LISTENING

LISTENING FOR TEXT ORGANIZATION FEATURES

8 👤 Students complete the exercise individually. Elicit the expressions from the class. Remind them that these are the kinds of phrases that they can use to structure their own talks in English, and that they will be given the opportunity to practise this language later in the unit.

> **Answers**
>
> 2 We will then discuss …
> 3 I'd like to start by talking (about) …
> 4 I'm going to (briefly) talk about …
> 5 Now, I'd like to mention …
> 6 In the next part of the lecture, I will discuss …

DISCUSSION

9 👤 Students make notes individually. For students that do not have a smartphone, ask them to recommend a particular piece of computer software (also sometimes now known as apps).

10 👥 Students complete the task in small groups. Allow 1–2 minutes per student.

Optional activity

If some of your students have smartphones, you could ask them to research ways that their phones could be used to help them learn English, both inside the classroom and outside. Tell them that they should focus on three aspects of smartphone use:

1 useful apps designed specifically for learners of English;

2 apps that provide useful practice but which were not designed primarily for learners of English (e.g. English language news apps, podcast apps, etc.);

3 ways that they can use their smartphones to use as the basis of discussion tasks (e.g. taking photographs of things they see during the week to discuss in class, taking photographs of their family to describe in class, etc.).

Students should be ready to talk about their ideas during the next class, and to recommend particular apps and tasks to the other students in the class.

CRITICAL THINKING

UNDERSTAND

1 👥 👥 Ask your class if any of them can remember life without the internet. Depending on their age and location, this may seem an amusing question. If you grew up without the internet, you could ask your students how they think that your life has changed since its creation. How do they think you prepared your classes, kept in contact with friends and colleagues, checked to see what the weather would be like later that day and researched travel destinations? Encourage discussion in the class to get them thinking a little about what things may have been like before the internet, then ask them to discuss the questions in pairs or small groups. Allow up to 5–10 minutes for discussion, and encourage the students to discuss all six questions in depth.

2 👤 Students complete the task individually. Set a time limit of 3–5 minutes, depending on the level and enthusiasm of the students.

3 👥 Students complete the task in small groups. Allow up to five minutes for discussion, then invite feedback from the class.

ANALYZE

4 👥 Students complete the task in pairs. Ask the students to write at least one question for each arm of the ideas map. Allow 2–4 minutes for the task, depending on the level of the class. If you have time, and internet access in the class, you could ask the students to research the answers to their questions. To make this research more challenging, you could assign this as a homework task and tell the students that they must not use the internet to find the answers, and to be ready to tell the class how well they were able to complete the task offline.

5 👥 Ask the pairs to each join another pair and allow up to five minutes for discussion. Rather than asking the students to show each other their questions, you could ask them to read the questions out and to see which of the two new students can answer first (or, if the students have had time to research the answers to the questions that they wrote, which student can first answer *correctly*). Monitor the groups as they answer each other's questions, then lead a class feedback session.

SPEAKING

PREPARATION FOR SPEAKING

OUTLINING A TOPIC

1 🔊 7.6 👤 Students complete the task individually and check their answers in pairs. You could ask them to first try to answer the questions based on what they think should be included in the introduction to a presentation, then check their answers against the recording.

2 👤👥 Give students 3–5 minutes to take brief notes individually, then ask them to each give the introduction to their partner once, who should give feedback. When both students per pair have given their introductions once, they should consider the feedback their partner gave and work this in to a second version of the introduction. Students give their introductions a second time and invite feedback from their partners.

ORGANIZING IDEAS

3 👤👥 Students complete the task individually or in pairs.

> **Answers**
> a 6 b 2 c 5 d 3 e 1 f 7 g 4

EXPLAINING HOW SOMETHING IS USED

4 👤 Students complete the task individually and check their answers in pairs.

> **Answers**
> 1 allows us 2 helps people to 3 is useful for
> 4 makes it 5 Without

5 👤 Students complete the task individually. Monitor the students as they write their sentences, giving feedback as appropriate.

6 👥 Students complete the task in pairs.

SPEAKING TASK

PREPARE

1 👤 Students complete the task individually. You could ask them to write down just one invention, then quickly elicit these from each student.

2 👤 Students complete the task individually. Ask them to write at least one question for each arm of the ideas map. Allow 2–4 minutes for the task, depending on the level of the class.

3 👥 Give the students up to five minutes to discuss their research questions and how they can use the internet most efficiently to find the answers.

After five minutes, elicit search strategies from the students and invite feedback or suggestions from the class. Then either allow time in class for the students to complete their research, or set the research and preparation of Exercise 4 as a homework task. Ask the students to prepare a presentation of 3–5 minutes, depending on the level of the class.

PRACTISE

4 👥 Students complete the task in pairs.

5 👥 Students complete the task in pairs.

PRESENT

6 👥 Ask the students to form new groups of three. Tell them that the groups should not include a pair who have already worked together during this class. Allow up to 3–5 minutes per presentation with 1–2 minutes for follow-up questions and answers. Tell the groups that each of the other students in the group must ask one question following each presentation. Quickly elicit a brief outline of each student's presentation. Then tell them to summarize the presentation in no more than two sentences.

TASK CHECKLIST AND OBJECTIVES REVIEW

Refer students to the end of each unit for the Task checklist and Objectives review. Students complete the tables individually to reflect on their learning and identify areas for improvement.

WORDLIST

See Teaching tips, pages 9–11 for ideas about how to make the most of the Wordlist with your students.

REVIEW TEST

See pages 110–111 for the photocopiable Review test for this unit, and page 91 for ideas about when and how to administer the Review test.

ADDITIONAL SPEAKING TASK

See page 124 for an Additional speaking task related to this unit.

Put students in groups of four or five. Focus them on the topic of the discussion. Explain that one student in each group should act as the chairperson. This person's job is to encourage other students to brainstorm ideas and give explanations, as well as to make sure that the presentation is planned in time.

Give students 10 minutes to plan their ideas. Go round and monitor to make sure students not only have 10 inventions, but are able to explain why they are important. When students have finished, ask each group to present their ideas to the rest of the class. Allow up to two minutes for each presentation. When each group has finished, round-up with the whole class and see if everyone can agree on the top three inventions of the last 100 years.

RESEARCH PROJECT

Invent and present a new mobile device.

Ask students to brainstorm all the different things mobile devices can do. Examples may include: calling friends and family, producing and editing films, creating music or making photo albums. In groups, ask students to think about what else they wish their mobile devices could do.

Each group should design a new device (which they can draw or piece together from other pictures) which allows them to do these new things. Each group can present their invention and vote for the best one. There are free online voting systems which allow you to do this. Search for 'voting software' to view some of these.

8 FASHION

Learning objectives

Before you start the *Unlock your knowledge* section, ask students to read the Learning objectives box. This will give them a clear idea of what they will learn in the unit. Tell them that you will return to these objectives at the end of the unit, when they review what they have learned. Give students the opportunity to ask any questions they might have.

UNLOCK YOUR KNOWLEDGE

Optional lead in

👥 Ask the class to write down the names of any designer-branded clothes that they are wearing (e.g. Levi's, Calvin Klein, Anita Dongre, etc.). For any shop-branded goods (e.g. Esprit, H&M, Gap, etc.), they should write down the name of the store where the item was bought. Give the students a strict time limit of one minute to do this, and tell them not to look at any of their labels – they must do the task from memory. Then ask the students to work in pairs and compare their lists. Invite comments from the class of which brands of clothing are the most popular.

👥👥 Students discuss questions 1–3 in small groups. Give the students up to three minutes, then elicit suggestions from some of the groups. Encourage class discussion; try to get a feel of how important fashion is to your students. Ask questions like: *What does your group think about fashion? Which brands are the most popular in your group? Does your group buy mainly designer-branded clothing or shop-branded clothing?* When discussing question 3, you could ask the students if there was ever a 'golden age' of fashion? Would they like to see a revival of some earlier fashions, such as the clothes that were popular in the 1960s or the 1980s?

WATCH AND LISTEN

▶ Video script

Fashion is important to a lot of people, but many of the clothes that are fashionable today didn't start as fashion items. Some clothes start as something practical and become fashionable as more people start to wear them.

For example, today, Missoni is a famous fashion house, known for its bold, bright patterns. But Missoni didn't start by making fashionable clothes.

Ottavio Missoni started Missoni fashion when he was young. He was an international athlete and made the tracksuits for the 1948 Olympics.

After his sporting career was over, he opened a workshop making woollen tracksuits. The Missoni family started making clothes with wool and now design other fashionable clothes.

Tracksuits also became fashion items and are popular because of the comfortable fit and fun colours.

Other fashion clothes started as sports clothes too. In the 1970s, jogging became popular and people needed more running shoes. By the 1980s, a lot of people owned running shoes and they wore them because they looked good and were comfortable. Celebrities started wearing them too. Running-shoe companies started to design shoes just for fashion and not for running, and they got famous sports stars to promote them.

Another fashion item we see every day is jeans. Jeans were invented by Levi Strauss. His first business sold tents and wagon covers to miners in California. The miners needed hard-wearing clothes and Strauss invented trousers for them made of canvas. Over the years he improved the design, adding rivets for strength, using a more comfortable denim material and dying the trousers dark blue to hide stains.

Up until the 1950s and 60s, jeans were worn by manual workers, like cowboys and steel workers, but they became really popular when movie stars such as Marlon Brando and James Dean started to wear them.

People started wearing jeans, not just for doing hard work, but as everyday clothes. So, the fashionable clothes you wear every day might have started from less stylish beginnings.

PREPARE TO WATCH

UNDERSTANDING KEY VOCABULARY

1 👤 Students complete the task individually and check their answers in pairs.

> **Answers**
> 1 tracksuits 2 denim 3 fashionable 4 patterns
> 5 woollen 6 practical 7 workshop 8 stains

PREDICTING CONTENT

2 👥 Give the students 3–5 minutes to complete the task in pairs. Elicit a few suggestions from the class, but do not comment in detail at this stage.

3 ▶ 👤 Students complete the task individually. Give the students a short time to discuss the questions following the recording, then elicit the answers from the students. Encourage class discussion, especially concerning question 1 where there might be some disagreement between students.

> **Answers**
> 1 Student's own answers, but could focus on things like jeans, sportswear, boots. The point in the video is that clothes originally designed for practicality often become fashionable.
> 2 for running/jogging, but also they can be worn for everyday use, because they have a comfortable fit
> 3 In the video, it suggests that they became popular in the 1980s because they looked good, were comfortable, and celebrities started to wear them.
> 4 They were invented for miners in California who needed hard-wearing clothes which also hid stains – they were worn originally by manual workers like cowboys and steel workers.

WHILE WATCHING

UNDERSTANDING MAIN IDEAS

4 ▶ 👤 Students complete the summary individually and check their answers in pairs. With a stronger group, you could ask the students to first try and complete the summary from memory before checking their suggested answers against the recording.

> **Answers**
> 1 stylish 2 Olympics 3 fit 4 jogging 5 celebrities 6 material

UNDERSTANDING DETAIL

5 ▶ 👤 Ask the students to read the sentences and to decide from memory whether they are true or false. Play the clip again and ask the students to check their answers. Quickly go through the answers with the class. With a stronger group, you could ask the students to rewrite the false sentences to make them correct (or to correct them orally).

> **Answers**
> 1 T 2 F 3 T 4 DNS 5 DNS 6 F 7 F 8 DNS

DISCUSSION

6 👥 Students discuss questions 1–5 in small groups. Give the students 3–5 minutes, then elicit ideas from some of the groups. If some of the questions have already been discussed during earlier tasks, you could ask the students to choose three questions to discuss.

LISTENING 1

PREPARING TO LISTEN

UNDERSTANDING KEY VOCABULARY

1 👤 Students complete the task individually and compare their answers in pairs. Quickly go through the answers with the class.

> **Optional activity**
>
> 👥 Ask the students to get into pairs (A & B) and tell them that they are going to perform a series of 60-second role-plays. You will call out the number of one of the statements from Exercise 1. Student A must read out the statement, Student B must respond and then the two students together must improvise a dialogue for 60 seconds. They must continue talking until you call out the next number for Student B to read out. Continue like this until you have called out all of the numbers, then quickly elicit summaries of some of the role-plays from the class.
>
> The most successful statements for this activity are: 1, 2, 5 and 6. The other statements can also be used, although they may demand a little more thought when setting a context for the dialogue.

> **Answers**
> 1 b 2 c 3 d 4 a 5 g 6 h 7 e 8 f 9 i

USING VISUALS TO PREDICT CONTENT

2 Ask the students to look at the photos and to try to guess what the focus of the discussion will be. Elicit ideas from the class, but do not comment at this stage.

3 👥 Give the students 5–10 minutes to read the predictions and discuss those that might come true. Ask them to give their reasons. For example, if they think that clothes will be able to reduce pain, how might this work? Why would it be desirable? Who could benefit from pain-reducing clothing? Why might this be preferable over conventional medicine, surgery and physiotherapy? Elicit some ideas from the class, but do not comment on whether or not they are correct. As a follow-up discussion task, you could ask the students to discuss in more detail those predictions that they think will not come true (e.g. why will they not come true?).

WHILE LISTENING

LISTENING FOR MAIN IDEAS

4 (◀) 8.1　👤 Students complete the task individually. Quickly go through the answers with the class.

> **Answers**
> 4, 6, 8, 9

PRONUNCIATION FOR LISTENING

> **Language note**
>
> Elision is when we do not pronounce a particular sound in a word, because it is affected by the following sound. Exercise 5 focuses on vowels that are unstressed when they appear between a consonant and /l/ or /r/, but there are many other examples of this phenomenon.
>
> Elision is one aspect of assimilation, which refers to the way a sound is affected by the sounds around it. This can cause the sound to disappear completely, or it can have a less drastic impact such as making a usually voiced sound become voiceless. For example, the /nd/ sound in *handbag* usually becomes something closer to an /m/ sound in rapid speech, so rather than saying /hændbæg/ we may say /hæmbæg/. In fact, to most people, the first pronunciation sounds overly articulated, and therefore rather artificial.

5 (◀) 8.2　👤👥 Students complete the task individually. You could ask the students to say the sentences out loud in pairs and discuss the possible answers before listening to the recording. If so, remind them not to overly articulate the words. They should try to sound as natural as possible. Go through the answers with the class. You could play each sentence individually so that the students can hear them again as you give them the respective answers.

> **Answers**
> 1 lib<u>r</u>ary 2 cam<u>e</u>ras 3 temp<u>e</u>rature 4 envi<u>r</u>onmentally 5 diff<u>e</u>rent

6 (◀) 8.2　👥 👥👥 Students then complete the task in pairs or small groups. If the class finds this aspect of pronunciation for listening difficult, have them work in groups of at least three.

LISTENING FOR DETAIL

7 (◀) 8.1　👤👥 Students complete the task individually or in pairs. With a stronger group, you could ask the students to try and answer the questions from memory first and then check their answers against the recording.

> **Answers**
> 1 a 2 b 3 b 4 b 5 c

8 👥 Ask the students to cover up definitions a-e with a piece of paper and to discuss the possible meanings of the words and phrases in bold. Elicit ideas for the definitions, but do not comment too much at this stage. Ask the students to look at a-e and to complete the task in pairs.

> **Answers**
> 1 c 2 a 3 e 4 b 5 d

POST-LISTENING

9 (◀) 8.3　👤 Students complete the task individually and check their answers in pairs.

> **Answers**
> 1a <u>That's</u> interesting.
> b That <u>is</u> interesting.
> 2a I've been <u>reading</u> about fashion in the future.
> b I <u>have</u> been reading about fashion in the future.
> 3a I agree that it's <u>not</u> very practical.
> b I <u>do</u> agree that it's not very practical.
> 4a I think that it'll be <u>interesting</u>.
> b I <u>do</u> think that it'll be interesting.

10 👥 👥👥 Students complete the task in pairs. If the class find pronunciation difficult, or have difficulty in producing appropriate stress and intonations patterns, have them work in groups of three. Give them two minutes to practise the sentences, then go through the answers with the class. As you go through the answers, you could model the correct pronunciation again and get the class to repeat the sentences after you until you are satisfied that everyone is stressing the correct words.

11 👥 Students complete the task in pairs. Once you have gone through the answers, get the pairs to repeat the sentences until they are sure that they are able to pronounce them correctly. You could then go through the sentences a second time with the class, modeling the correct stress and asking the class to repeat the sentences in a chorus.

Answers

1 I do believe they can be used to make sports clothing.
2 I does seem we have a lot of ideas for the future of fashion.
3 I do agree.
4 I do like the idea of clothes that help people with health problems.
5 She does buy a lot of clothes.

DISCUSSION

12 👥 Students complete the task in pairs. Note that question 3 could be understood on several levels:

- *Why do some particular people have to be fashionable? (e.g. celebrities)*
- *Why do some people like to be fashionable?*

You could either go through these different meanings with your students, or allow them to interpret the sentence as they wish.

⊙ LANGUAGE DEVELOPMENT

IDIOMS AND FIXED EXPRESSIONS

Language note

An idiom is a fixed expression that cannot easily be understood from looking at its individual words. For example, in the expression *Can you give me a hand?* the speaker does not literally want the other person to give him or her a hand, the speaker is simply asking for help. The entire expression has a fixed meaning that is understood by most people. These kinds of fixed expressions are referred to as *idioms*, a term used to refer to fixed expressions that people approve of.

A cliché is a saying or remark that is very often made and is therefore not original and not interesting. It is a saying that has been so overused that it is no longer fresh. These sayings can be phrases that are

especially common or fashionable at any one time (e.g. *to be honest*), they can be proverbs (e.g. *don't put all your eggs in one basket*), they can be similes (e.g. *As daft as a brush*) or they can be single words (e.g. *Whatever*). The word cliché is used to refer to fixed expressions that many speakers and writers do not approve of.

It is not always easy to know whether something is an acceptable fixed expression, or whether it is considered a cliché. As a rough guide, the more colourful or idiomatic an expression is, the more likely it is to be a cliché. However, this is a rather blunt definition. To a certain extent, whether or not something is to be considered a cliché will be down to the judgment of the individual.

When choosing idiomatic language to teach, we should consider very carefully whether this language is still actively used (e.g. *As far as I'm concerned*), or dated expressions that are less likely to be in active use (e.g. *It's raining cats and dogs*, etc.). It is always tempting to include examples of this language in our lessons as they can be fun to teach, and our students often enjoy learning them. However, we do them a disservice if we actively teach them to use clichés. Idiomatic language that is not clichéd is useful for our students to know and use. However, clichéd language should be, as one old joke has it, *avoided like the plague*!

1 👥 Students discuss the possible meanings in pairs. Elicit some ideas from the class, but do not feed back in detail at this stage.

2 👤👥 Students complete the task individually or in pairs. Elicit the answers from the class.

Answers

a As far as I'm concerned
b at long last
c just for the fun of it
d mad about
e and all that
f give me a hand
g dying to
h as long as

Optional activity

Once the class is clear as to the meaning of the fixed expressions in Exercises 1 and 2, ask the students to look at them again and underline those they would feel most comfortable using. They should then practise using these during a discussion with a partner (either one of the discussion tasks from the book, or a topic of their own choice). The aim of the discussion is to try and sound as natural as possible when using the fixed expressions.

TALKING ABOUT THE FUTURE

> ## Language note
>
> There are many ways of talking about the future in English. Exercises 1–4 illustrate some of the most common. The notes below offer a brief explanation together with some more examples. More information and examples can be found online by typing *talking about the future* into a search engine.
>
> When we know what is going to happen in the future, for example when something has already been decided, or when something is obviously going to happen, we usually use the *present tense*.
>
> We often use the Present continuous for plans we have made (e.g. *I'm leaving this afternoon*).
>
> We often use *be going + infinitive* for plans we have made, especially when talking informally (e.g. *We're going to the cinema tonight*).
>
> We also use *be going + infinitive* where we can see that something will obviously happen, or that it is very likely (e.g. *It's going to rain*).
>
> We can use the Present simple for timetables and schedules (e.g. *The train leaves at 7:54 in the morning*).
>
> We use *will* for decisions made at the time of speaking (e.g.
> A: *The motorway is closed this morning.*
> B: *OK, we'll take the scenic route*).
>
> *Will* is also used to make predictions (e.g. *You'll have a great time!*) and to make offers and promises (e.g. *I'll write soon*).

3 Students complete the task individually or in pairs. Elicit the answers from the class.

> ### Answers
> 2 will 3 are playing 4 will 5 is leaving 6 is going to

4 Students complete the task individually and check their answers with a partner. Elicit the answers from the class.

> ### Answers
> a we are having (present continuous)
> b arrives (present simple)
> c it's going to rain (going to)
> d I'll be (will)

5 Students complete the task individually and check their answers with a partner.

> ### Answers
> 1 am flying / am going to fly
> 2 starts
> 3 are going to be
> 4 will stay

LISTENING 2

PREPARING TO LISTEN

UNDERSTANDING KEY VOCABULARY

1 Students complete the task individually and check their answers with a partner. Elicit the answers from the class.

> ### Answers
> a admired b modest c unique d collection
> e individual f combine g confidence h trend

USING YOUR KNOWLEDGE

2 Give the students 2–4 minutes to discuss the questions in pairs or small groups. Elicit ideas from the class. You could first organize the groups by asking those who like the clothes in the picture to stand on one side of the room and those who don't like them on the other. Students should then arrange themselves into pairs or small groups with including at least one student from each side of the room.

WHILE LISTENING

LISTENING FOR MAIN IDEAS

3 ◀)) 8.4 Students complete the task individually and check their answers with a partner. Elicit the answers from the class.

> ### Answers
> 1 She is a fashion designer.
> 2 Qatar
> 3 unique designs which combined tradition Muslim fashion with French chic

4 ◀)) 8.5 Ask the students to guess which of the topics will be mentioned before listening to the recording. Then play the recording and ask them to check their answers.

LISTENING FOR DETAIL

5 ◀)) 8.5 Students complete the task individually and check their answers with a partner. Elicit the answers from the class. Again, you could first ask the students to try and guess what the answers will be before they listen to the next part of the interview.

This will be especially useful for weaker students, and will help ensure that they have first read and understood the statements.

Answers
1 F 2 T 3 T 4 DNS 5 T 6 T 7 T 8 F 9 F

DISCUSSION

6 👥 Students complete the task in small groups. If you feel that the class has already covered some of these questions, ask the groups to choose the two or three questions that most interest them. Allow 3–5 minutes for discussion, then briefly elicit feedback from each group.

CRITICAL THINKING

APPLY

1 👤 Students complete the task individually and check their answers with a partner.

Answers
1 F 2 F 3 F 4 A 5 A 6 F

2 👤👥 Students tick the opinions individually and discuss their answers with a new partner. Allow up two five minutes for the students to explain their answers in detail. Then quickly elicit one or two thoughts on each question from the class. This is a good opportunity to encourage class discussion, although this may depend on the students' own experience of wearing a uniform either at work or at school. You could also set this task up as a group task.

> **Language note**
>
> The term *devil's advocate* is used to describe someone who pretends, in an argument or discussion, to be against an idea or plan that a lot of people support, in order to make people discuss and consider it in more detail. It is most commonly used in the expression *to play* devil's advocate: *I don't really believe all that – I was just playing devil's advocate*. Playing devil's advocate is a good way to test the strength of the opposing arguments.

ANALYZE

3 👤👥 Ask the students to read the dialogue. You could ask them to briefly discuss whether or not they agree with B's argument in pairs.

Quickly elicit comments on the way the point of view is raised and on the strength of the argument.

Answers
Speaker B accepts A's point of view, but then raises a counter-argument, giving an example.

4 👤 Students complete the task individually. Point out that there is sometimes more than one possible answer.

Possible answers
a 2 b 1, 6 c 4 d 1, 6 e 6 f 3 g 6

EVALUATE

5 👥 Remind students of the expression *to play devil's advocate*. Ask them to first read the opinions individually and write 'A' (=agree) or 'D' (=disagree) by the side of each argument. Then give them 1–2 minutes to think of one alternative point of view for each of the opinions they agree with. Once they are ready, ask the students in pairs to take it in turns to choose one opinion they agree with and then to give an alternative point of view. Allow 3–5 minutes for this part of the task, then quickly elicit one alternative point of view for each opinion (if possible – it may be that all of the class disagree with one or more of the opinions). You could also ask the students to think of alternative points of view for those opinions with which they disagree.

SPEAKING

PREPARATION FOR SPEAKING

1 👤 Ask the students to read the information box on indirect questions and then to answer the questions individually. Give them 2–4 minutes to complete the exercise, depending on their level, then ask them to compare their ideas in pairs. Elicit the answers from the class.

Answers
1 questions e, g
2 questions a, c, e, g

2 Students complete the task individually and check their answers with a partner.

> **Answers**
> 1 What do you think 2 Would you say that
> 3 Don't you agree 4 Do you mean that

FOCUSING ON INFORMATION THAT FOLLOWS

3 8.6 Students complete the task individually and check their answers with a partner. Point out that the first question has been done as an example. You could tell the students that this kind of language is useful for two reasons: it gives the speaker a little more time to think about what it is they want to say; it helps prepare the listener for what is about to be said.

> **Answers**
> 2 Let me give you an example
> 3 As far as I'm concerned
> 4 My feeling is this
> 5 What I think it that
> 6 Another thing is that

4 8.6 Play the recording again and elicit the reason for the short pause from the class.

> **Answers**
> To create a gap between the focusing phrase and the real content.

5 Students complete the task in pairs. Give the students up to three minutes for the role-play, then elicit some of the opinions and arguments expressed from the class.

6 Students complete the task in pairs. Give the students up to three minutes for the role-play. You could briefly elicit one or two further opinions.

SPEAKING TASK

PREPARE

1 Ask the class to read the notes at the top of the page and to find out what the speaking task is (to take part in an interview to find out attitudes towards uniforms and dress codes). Allow 3–5 minutes for the students to complete the task in small groups. Quickly elicit one or two ideas for each of the three questions.

2 Students complete this stage of the task individually. Have two students take the same role if necessary, in which case they should prepare the task together. Give the students two minutes to take notes. Ask the interviewers to prepare some interesting questions and to be ready to follow up any answers with further questions. Tell the interviewees to be ready to give detailed answers, explaining and justifying their opinions with examples and further detail where possible.

PRACTISE

3 Students complete this stage of the task in pairs (A + B; C + D). Allow 5–10 minutes for the interview, depending on how well prepared the students are/the level of the class. Elicit brief summaries of the discussions from one or two sets of pairs.

4 Students complete the task in pairs. Remind the class that the criticism should be constructive, so that their partners have a good idea as to where and how they can improve. At the end of the feedback session, give the students 1–2 minutes to amend their notes ready for the next interview.

DISCUSS

5 Students complete the task in pairs. Allow 5–10 minutes for the interview, then elicit brief summaries of the discussions from one or two sets of pairs.

TASK CHECKLIST AND OBJECTIVES REVIEW

Refer students to the end of each unit for the Task checklist and Objectives review. Students complete the tables individually to reflect on their learning and identify areas for improvement.

WORDLIST

See Training tips, pages 9–11 for ideas about how to make the most of the Wordlist with your students.

REVIEW TEST

See pages 112–113 for the photocopiable Review test for this unit, and page 91 for ideas about when and how to administer the Review test.

ADDITIONAL SPEAKING TASK

See page 125 for an Additional speaking task related to this unit.

Put students in groups of four. Explain that they are going to take part in a TV discussion show on the theme of fashion. Ask students to read their role cards (A, B, C or D) and to make notes on their information for two minutes.

Next, put students together to role-play the discussion. Allow the interaction to continue for up to 10 minutes. Go round and monitor students' abilities to ask for and give opinions and information.

RESEARCH PROJECT

Design and present clothes for the future.

Ask students to think about different environments that people live in, e.g. indoor, rainy or hot. Now ask them to think about different types of clothing and accessories for different parts of the body like hats, jackets, watches, trousers and bags. Then ask them to imagine how these clothes could be designed to help people in their environment, e.g. a hat may have a cooling system to help people keep cool, or a watch could be a communication device.

Students could use tools on the Cambridge LMS to share ideas. In groups, ask students to design and present an item of 'smart' clothing or an accessory like the ones they have been thinking about. As an additional activity, one group could interview another group about their design and upload this to the forum on the Cambridge LMS as a podcast. (Search for 'how to create a podcast', for more information. Audio recordings should be saved as 128kb mp3 files.)

9 ECONOMICS

UNLOCK YOUR KNOWLEDGE

👥👥 Students discuss the questions in small groups. For question 3, you could ask students to extend the discussion to the kinds of things people their age like to spend money on. Allow five minutes for discussion, then elicit ideas from the class. Encourage discussion, especially if any potentially contentious statements are made.

WATCH AND LISTEN

▶ Video script

During the last few decades, an economic revolution has taken place in China. In Chinese cities, economic regulations have been relaxed and people are buying, selling and building to make money.

The result is the biggest economic migration in world history, as tens of millions of Chinese move from the countryside to urban areas in search of wealth and success.

Sun Feng came to Shanghai from his village a year ago. He is not alone: of a population of 20 million, over three million people in Shanghai are migrant workers. However, the only job he could find was one of the most dangerous in the city.

He is a window cleaner, washing the city's skyscrapers. It is terrifying work.

Sun Feng would like to buy a car, but the ones in this showroom are a fantasy for him. He must save the small amount of money he earns to feed his wife and baby daughter back in his home village.

High above the Shanghai streets at night, Sun Feng is still hard at work. Many Chinese companies want their windows cleaned at night so their workers are not disturbed during the day.

Sun Feng is unsure about the rich new world full of luxuries he has found in Shanghai. He believes that if China continues to develop economically, the country will lose some of its traditional, simple culture.

It is the Chinese New Year and Sun Feng is going back to his village to celebrate. When he left home, his daughter was a baby and he hasn't seen her for a year. He misses her.

It is one of the many sacrifices he has made by moving to Shanghai, following the economic dream of millions of Chinese people hoping for a better life.

PREPARING TO WATCH

UNDERSTANDING KEY VOCABULARY

1 👤 Students complete the task individually and check their answers in pairs. Quickly go through the answers with the class.

> **Answers**
> 1 b 2 c 3 a 4 b 5 a 6 c 7 b 8 a

USING VISUALS TO PREDICT CONTENT

2 👥 Give the students 3–5 minutes to discuss the task in pairs, then elicit ideas from the class. Encourage the students to support their ideas with evidence from the photographs and the extract from the video.

3 ▶👤 Students complete the task individually and check their answers in pairs. Quickly elicit the answers from the class.

WHILE WATCHING

UNDERSTANDING MAIN IDEAS

4 ▶👤 Students complete the task individually and compare their answers in pairs. With stronger groups, you could ask them first to try to answer the questions from memory before watching the video again to check and complete their answers. Quickly elicit the answers from the class.

> **Answers**
> 1 to earn money to feed his wife and baby daughter back in his home village
> 2 a window cleaner
> 3 no, it is dangerous
> 4 once a year

UNDERSTANDING DETAIL

5 👤 Students complete the task individually and compare their answers in pairs. Again, with stronger groups, you could ask them first to try to answer the questions from memory before watching the video again to check and complete their answers. Quickly elicit the answers from the class.

> **Answers**
> 1 T 2 T 3 F 4 F 5 T 6 T

DISCUSSION

6 👥 Give the students up to five minutes to discuss the questions in small groups, then elicit ideas from the class. Encourage sensitive discussion on this issue. Some of your students may have string pro- or anti-immigrant feelings, so make sure to keep the discussion reasoned. Ask the students to support their views with evidence and concrete examples rather than anecdotal second-hand views and received wisdom. You may have the children of immigrant workers in your class, in which case they may be prepared to share some of their own experiences with the class.

LISTENING 1

PREPARING TO LISTEN

UNDERSTANDING KEY VOCABULARY

1 👤 Students complete the task individually and check their answers in pairs. Quickly elicit the answers from the students.

> **Answers**
> 1 results of this survey 2 save money 3 Luxury cars
> 4 invested all his money 5 can't afford to 6 loan
> 7 debt to pay 8 wealthy 9 worth a lot of money
> 10 waste your money

USING YOUR KNOWLEDGE

2 👥 Students complete the task in pairs. Allow 2–4 minutes for discussion, then elicit ideas from the class. You could first ask the students what they understand by the term *millionaire* (see language note below).

> **Language note**
>
> Most dictionaries define a *millionaire* as a person whose assets (money and property) are worth at least one million pounds, dollars or euros, etc. However, the term *millionaire* is often used more colloquially to refer to a very rich person, usually one who earns lots of money as well as being asset rich. In countries such as the UK, this can be an important distinction as it is quite possible for someone to be asset rich (e.g. because they own a house in central London, where property prices have risen dramatically over the past few decades) but who does not earn the kind of income that would finance the typical view of a millionaire lifestyle.
>
> Although the term *millionaire* is most closely associated with relatively strong currencies such as the pound, the dollar and the euro, countries with other currencies often use versions of the term to refer to very rich people. For example, the term *Millionär* was in common use in Austria before it became part of the eurozone (the economic region made up of countries that have adopted the euro as currency), and was used to mean very rich. This was despite the fact that a person who has assets of at least one million Austrian schillings was worth 20 times less than someone who had assets of at least one million British pounds.
>
> It would be worth finding out from your students what they understand by the term *millionaire* in English, whether or not they use a similar term in their first language, and how that term is defined.

3 🔊 9.1 👥👥 Students listen to the recording and discuss the questions in pairs or small groups. Set a strict time limit of two minutes for the discussion, then quickly elicit ideas from the class. Point out that *wealthy* means 'rich' – but it can also mean the feeling of having what you need. For example, a person doesn't have to have lots of money to feel wealthy if he or she has lots of friends, a good family, a comfortable place to live, etc.

WHILE LISTENING

LISTENING FOR MAIN IDEAS

4 👥 Give the students three minutes to discuss the statements in small groups and decide which ones are true. Encourage them to explain their reasoning in detail. Why do they think that a particular statement is/is not true? Elicit ideas from the class and ask the students to support their answers with examples where possible.

Optional activity

👥 You could also set this up as a pair-work ranking activity. Ask the students to work on their own and number the statements 1–8; 1=most true, 8=least true. When they have finished ranking the statements, ask them to discuss their ranking in pairs and to agree on a common ranking.

5 🔊 9.2 👤 Students complete the task individually and check their answers in pairs.

Answers

The following are true, according to the recording: 2, 3, 4, 5, 7.

6 👥 Give the students 2–3 minutes to discuss their ideas in pairs, then elicit suggestions from the class.

PRONUNCIATION FOR LISTENING

Language note

Silent letters are those letters that do not correspond to any sound when the word is said out loud. These are a feature of many languages, although English is noted as having a particularly high number of silent letters. This can create difficulties for both native and non-native speakers of English, as it makes it more difficult to spell certain words.

Your students might be interested to know why there are so many silent letters in English.

Consonant clusters are sometimes simplified where once they were pronounced in full (e.g. there used to be a silent th in Christmas).

Compound words are sometimes simplified to make them easier to pronounce. As with consonant clusters, the spelling often stay the same (e.g. cupboard, which contains a silent p, but was once fully articulated as cup and board).

Letters have been inserted into the spelling at different periods of the development of modern English. For example, the silent b in debt was deliberately inserted to reflect the word's Latin origin (debitum) via Old French. Some of the silent h sounds that are common in English words such as ghost were inserted by Dutch-speaking typesetters, reflecting the spelling of their own first language.

Other changes in pronunciation can also leave some letters redundant. For example, the gh was once pronounced in words such as light, but is no longer spoken.

7 👥 Students complete the task in pairs. Point out that the bolded words all contain letters that are not pronounced. You could

elicit some or all of the sentences from the students, although this would pre-empt the next task. One way to deal with this would be to elicit the sentences from individual students and then ask the rest of the class whether or not they think that the sentence was correctly pronounced. Where the class disagrees, invite another student to try. Do not comment on whether or not the pronunciation is correct, but tell the students that they will hear the correct pronunciation in the next listening task. They can then see which student (if any) pronounced the sentence(s) correctly.

8 🔊 9.3 👥 👥👥 Students listen to the sentences and discuss the correct pronunciation of the words in bold in pairs or small groups. Elicit the correct pronunciation of the bolded words from the class. Once the class is clear on which letters are silent, you could play each sentence one last time, stopping at the end of each sentence and inviting the class to repeat the sentence until you are certain that everyone is pronouncing them correctly.

Answers

1 surprising   2 yacht   3 exactly   4 designer   5 debt
6 doubt   7 answer

LISTENING FOR DETAIL

9 🔊 9.2 👤 Students complete the task individually. With a stronger group, you could ask the students to try to answer the questions from memory before checking their answers against the recording.

Answers

1 75% (not half)
2 Half (not 60%)
3 65% (not 33%)
4 86% (not 68%)
5 married (not single)

POST-LISTENING

10 👤 👥 Students complete the task individually or in pairs. Quickly go through the answers with the class. You could also deal with this question quickly as a class activity.

Answers

1 b   2 c

11 👤👥 Students complete the task individually or in pairs. Quickly go through the answers with the class. You could also deal with this question quickly as a class activity.

> **Answers**
> 1 a 2 c

DISCUSSION

12 👤 Students complete the task individually. You could ask them to put the five statements into the order in which they most agree with them: 1 = agree with the most; 2 = agree with the least. Give the students five minutes to take notes in preparation for the discussion.

13 👥 Students complete the task in small groups. Allow 5–10 minutes for the discussion, monitor the groups and take notes for later feedback. Elicit ideas from the class, focusing on what each group thinks is the most important lesson. You could lead a class discussion in which the class tries to agree on which is the single most important lesson.

◉ LANGUAGE DEVELOPMENT

COLLOCATIONS WITH *PAY, SAVE* AND *MONEY*

> **Language note**
>
> Collocations are combinations of words formed when two or more words are often used together in a way that sounds correct to people who have spoken the language all their lives, but might not be expected from the meaning. It is useful for your students to learn collocations as it will help them express their ideas much more naturally. For example, a non-native speaker may describe traffic as being *strong*. However, the correct collocation is *heavy traffic*, a combination of words that is not necessarily immediately obvious to learners, but which is typical of native speakers of English. It is useful for students to record the most common collocations around particular verbs or nouns, as learning collocations thematically can help them remember the most important word combinations.

1 👤👥 Students complete the task individually or in pairs. Quickly go through the answers with the class.

> **Answers**
> **save** time; energy
> **pay** attention; someone a visit; a fine
> spend; make; earn **money**

2 👤 Students complete the task individually. Quickly go through the answers with the class.

> **Answers**
> 1 spent 2 making 3 save 4 paying 5 pay 6 lost
> 7 save 8 borrowed 9 save 10 paid

CONDITIONAL SENTENCES

3 👤👥 Ask the students to read the information box on conditional sentences and to complete the task individually or in pairs. Elicit the answers from the class.

> **Answers**
> a 1, 4 b 2, 3

4 👤 Students complete the task individually and check their answers in pairs. Quickly go through the answers with the class.

> **Answers**
> 1 If you want to spend money, don't buy lots of expensive things.
> 2 If you have time, listen to this radio programme.
> 3 If I have money, I always buy new clothes.
> 4 If you pay off all your debts, you will be happier.

> **Optional activity**
>
> You could turn this error-correction activity into a game by adopting the easy first procedure, a technique that works especially well when you have two or more short exercises together. Write the question numbers on the board and ask the students to complete the exercise in teams. When the teams have finished answering the questions, ask the first team to choose the number of a question that they are sure they can answer correctly. If the team answers the question correctly, circle the question number with the team's colour and move on to the next team. Continue like this until all of the questions have been answered. The team with the most numbers at the end is the winner.

5 👤 Students complete the task individually and discuss their answers in pairs.

Optional activity
If you have a larger class, you could make the exercise last a little longer by adding these sentences.
If you are happy, …
If you need to lose weight, …
If you want to pass your English exam, …
If you learn the common collocations, …
If you can't sleep, …
If you lose your mobile, …
If you can't drive, …
If you lose touch with friends, …
If you have a credit card, …
If you travel regularly, …

LISTENING 2

PREPARING TO LISTEN

UNDERSTANDING KEY VOCABULARY

1 👤 Students complete the task individually and compare their answers in pairs. Quickly go through the answers with the class.

> **Answers**
> 1 i 2 h 3 g 4 c 5 d 6 e 7 f 8 a 9 j 10 b

USING YOUR KNOWLEDGE

2 🔊 9.4 👥 Students listen to the introduction to the discussion and complete the table in small groups. You could also ask them to first brainstorm as many ideas for or against and then decide on the best ones. If so, remind your students that during the first part of a brainstorming session the aim is to get as many ideas as possible, good or bad. Students should not comment on each other's ideas at this stage, they should simply note them down. Once a brainstorming session has led to lots of ideas, the merits of these ideas can then be discussed in detail. Allow 5–10 minutes for detailed discussion, then ask each group to give you their best idea for and their best idea against. Continue like this, noting the ideas on the board. Go back to the first group and repeat the procedure until all of the best ideas have been collected.

WHILE LISTENING

LISTENING FOR CONTRASTING VIEWPOINTS

3 🔊 9.5 👤 Students complete the task individually. Quickly elicit the answers from the class.

> **Answers**
> 1 F 2 A 3 A

4 🔊 9.5 👤 Students complete the task individually. With a stronger group, you could ask the students to try to answer the questions from memory before checking their answers against the recording.

> **Answers**
> 1 c 2 b 3 c 4 a 5 b 6 a

POST-LISTENING

5 👤👥 Students complete the task individually or in pairs. Quickly elicit the answers from the class.

> **Answers**
> 1 b 2 a 3 b

6 👤👥 Students complete the task individually or in pairs. Elicit the answers from the class and remind the students that this kind of language is useful in discussions as it helps prepare the listener for what the speaker is about to say.

> **Answers**
> 1 I understand; I can see your point; I realize that
> 2 However; but; but

DISCUSSION

7 👤 Give the students up to three minutes to take notes on the questions. You could remind them of the arguments for and against that were discussed earlier, and ask them to look at these again and decide which ones they most agree with. Point out that good answers to questions 2 and 3 are especially important in preparing a discussion, and will make their opinions sound much more authoritative and persuasive.

8 👥 Students complete the task in small groups. As this discussion should lead to a clear decision, you could appoint a chair and a secretary for each group. The chair should start the meeting and confirm its aims. They should then ensure that everyone gets an equal chance to put forward their views. The secretary should take notes on what is said, and is responsible for correctly noting down the final decision. Give the students up to 10 minutes to complete the task, then invite the secretaries to present the groups' decision. Appointing a chair and a secretary helps give a discussion a more formal tone, and is more likely to lead to a clear decision on which the whole group can agree.

CRITICAL THINKING

UNDERSTAND

1 👥 Students complete the task in pairs. Give the students up to five minutes to discuss the questions, then quickly elicit some ideas from the class. Once you have an overview of the different attitudes represented by the class, you could lead a class discussion based on question 4.

2 (◀ 9.6) 👤 Students complete the task individually. Quickly elicit the answers from the class.

> **Answers**
>
> Joseph: against, children should be taught that it's their responsibility to do work as family members
> Karen: against, children shouldn't think that they receive money from their parents
> Robert: for, it's good to give children a little money – it teaches them about maths.

3 👥 Students complete the task in small groups. Monitor the discussions and take notes on the students' language for later feedback. Allow 2–4 minutes discussion time, then lead a brief feedback session based on the language you have noted. You could also briefly elicit some opinions based on what the students have heard.

ANALYZE

4 👤 Give the students 2–4 minutes to take notes on their roles. You could also ask them to anticipate the arguments that their partner is likely to put forward during the discussion, and to prepare brief notes on possible counterarguments.

CREATE

5 👥 Students complete the task in pairs. Allow up to five minutes for discussion. Remind them to use conditional language and the language used when presenting and discussing opinions. Monitor the groups and give feedback on the students' language at the end of the task.

SPEAKING

PREPARATION FOR SPEAKING

1 👤👥 Ask the class to read the explanation box and to complete the task individually or in pairs. Elicit the answers from the class.

> **Answers**
>
> 1 Learning
> 2 Saving money
> 3 Reading books about millionaires
> 4 Teaching children about money

2 👤👥 Students complete the task individually or in pairs. Point out that the first question has been done as an example. Elicit the answers from the class.

> **Answers**
>
> 2 Paying children to study can encourage them.
> 3 Learning about money is difficult when you're a child.
> 4 Giving children money at an early age can spoil them.
> 5 Teaching children to save money is very important.

3 👥 Students complete the task in pairs. Ask them to write the sentences down, monitor the pairs and give feedback as appropriate. Try to review at least one sentence written by each pair and give any necessary corrections. Then elicit one correct sentence from each pair.

4 (◀ 9.7) 👤 Ask the students to read the phrases first. Students then complete the task individually. Quickly elicit the answers from the class.

Optional activity

👥 👥👥 Exercise 4 presents some useful language for asking for more information. There are other ways to do this.

Ask the class to give you an example of another expression that could be used to ask for more information. Give feedback and continue asking until you have elicited one correct alternative phrase (e.g. *You really think so?*). Then point out that without even speaking there are other ways to ask for more information, or to show that you don't understand. Elicit one of these ways from the students. If necessary, give an example (e.g. frowning). You could tell the students that some of these non-linguistic ways may be culturally specific, and that a common example of body language in one country may not be understood, or may be understood differently, in another country. Students then work in pairs or small groups and think of other linguistic and non-linguistic ways of asking someone to explain more. Give the students five minutes to think of ways of asking someone to explain more, elicit suggestions from the class and give feedback.

5 👥👥 Students complete the task in small groups. Remind them that they should ask each other to explain their reasons. Monitor the discussions and take notes on the students' language for later feedback. Allow 5–10 minutes discussion time, then elicit some opinions from the students. Ask them to explain their reasons using some of the language presented earlier in the unit. You could also ask the students to explain their ideas further by using facial expressions and body language.

SPEAKING TASK

PREPARE

Optional activity

Ask the class to read the topic of the debate and to quickly decide for themselves whether or not teenagers should have credit cards. Then tell the students that you are going to ask those who believe that teenagers should have credit cards to raise their hands, and those who think that they should not to raise their books. Tell them to be ready with a decision, and that on the count of three they should raise their hands or books. Countdown from three, and comment briefly on the result.

1 👥👥 Ask the students to read the news story and to find out why the topic of allowing teenagers to have credit cards is a matter of public debate (many teenagers get into debt). Elicit the answer, then ask students to discuss the questions in small groups. You could also ask them to discuss the benefits of having a credit card, and the difficulties encountered by not having one. Allow five minutes for discussion, then elicit ideas from the class. If not already discussed during the feedback session, you could ask those with a credit card to tell you how different their lives would be if they did not have one.

2 👤 Give the students three minutes to write notes on as many advantages and disadvantages of giving teenagers credit cards as they can.

3 👥 Students complete the task in pairs. Allow 2–4 minutes for this discussion.

4 👤 Students complete the task individually. Allow up to five minutes for the students to take detailed notes.

PRACTISE

5 👥👥 Ask the students to form groups of four. Allow 10 minutes for detailed discussion. Remind the students to give reasons and examples, and to ask the other students in their groups to explain their reasons in more detail (when more detail is needed).

6 👥👥 Students complete the task in their groups. Remind the class that their discussion should be constructive, and that the students should each be left with a clear idea as to their strengths and those aspects of their language of discussion that could be improved.

DISCUSS

7 and 8 👥👥 Students complete the task in new groups. Allow 5–10 minutes for discussion, then ask one person from each group to present their group's opinions.

TASK CHECKLIST AND OBJECTIVES REVIEW

Refer students to the end of each unit for the Task checklist and Objectives review. Students complete the tables individually to reflect on their learning and identify areas for improvement.

WORDLIST

See Teaching tips, pages 9–11 for ideas about how to make the most of the Wordlist with your students.

REVIEW TEST

See pages 114–115 for the photocopiable Review test for this unit, and page 91 for ideas about when and how to administer the Review test.

ADDITIONAL SPEAKING TASK

See page 126 for an Additional speaking task related to this unit.

Put students in groups of four or five. Introduce the debate topic. Students have been asked to contribute to a discussion to create ideas for new ways to raise taxes. Focus students on the questions and allow up to two minutes for them to make notes.

Then, allow up to 10 minutes for students to discuss their ideas. It may be helpful for each group to appoint a chairperson, to ensure that everyone gets a chance to speak.

When the students have finished, round up by getting feedback from the whole class.

RESEARCH PROJECT

Create an eBook to help people budget their finances.

Divide the class into groups. Ask each group to search for 'budget your finances'. Give each group a different area to focus on, e.g. how to save money, how to create a budget, why it is important to budget. Students should make a note of their findings – they could use tools on the Cambridge LMS, for example the blog or wiki, for this.

Tell the class they will be creating a class eBook using the information they have gathered (you can find guides and eBook software by searching for 'create eBook'). Each group will write a different section based on their research area, including information, advice and explanations of any specialist financial vocabulary.

THE BRAIN

Learning objectives

Before you start the *Unlock your knowledge* section, ask students to read the Learning objectives box. This will give them a clear idea of what they will learn in the unit. Tell them that you will return to these objectives at the end of the unit, when they review what they have learned. Give students the opportunity to ask any questions they might have.

UNLOCK YOUR KNOWLEDGE

Optional activity

Draw a sketch of a human brain on the board, or display one on a projector. Elicit the topic of the lesson from the class (the brain). Give the class 60 seconds to discuss what they know about the brain in pairs. Then ask the students if any of them could talk for 60 seconds on their own about the same topic. Encourage one student to be a 'volunteer'. Tell that student that you would like them to talk about the brain without pausing, without repeating any words and without going off-topic. Ask the other students to 'challenge' if they hear the speaker do any of these three things. If a student correctly challenges, they continue speaking on the topic. As soon as 60 seconds have passed, ask the students to work in groups of four and to try the activity themselves. Each student in each group of four should have the chance to begin one of these topics:

- the brain
- the mind
- intelligence
- personality.

👥 👥👥 Students discuss the questions in pairs or small groups. Allow five minutes for discussion, then elicit ideas from the class. Encourage class discussion and try to establish the difference between the mind and the brain.

WATCH AND LISTEN

▶ Video script

Kate, a psychology student, is taking part in an experiment to test her brain's ability to respond to pain. She is going to be burned on her forearm without any painkillers.

Her Professor, Tor Wager, places a metal plate the temperature of a very hot cup of coffee on her forearm. It is an uncomfortable experiment, designed to investigate the placebo effect.

The placebo effect occurs in the brain when a person is told that something will improve their health, or a painful condition, and they get better. However, nothing has actually been given or done to them to physically alter their condition.

Doctor Wager thinks that the power of suggestion actually produces a physical change in the brain, which is why placebo medicines can seem to have the same effects as real drugs.

His plan is to look for changes in the part of the brain that senses pain while Kate is burned with the metal plate. Kate enters a scanner. The professor burns her arm again and the scanner records her brain activity while she is in pain.

Professor Wager then puts a cream on Kate's skin. He tells her that it is a powerful pain killer, but the lotion is a placebo. It is body cream, with nothing in it to stop the pain from the burns. Kate enters the scanner again and she is burned at exactly the same temperature as before.

This time, however, there is not as much activity in the pain centre of her brain. Kate actually feels a lot less pain, even though the lotion on her skin is not a painkiller.

The experiments show that the human brain's ability to recognize pain is flexible, as it can physically respond to a placebo by changing its signals. It seems the placebo effect really can work.

BEFORE WATCHING

UNDERSTANDING KEY VOCABULARY

1 👤 Students complete the task individually and check their answers in pairs.

> **Answers**
>
> 1 experiment 2 respond 3 burned 4 seem to
> 5 painkiller 6 ability 7 occur 8 alter

USING YOUR KNOWLEDGE TO PREDICT CONTENT

2 👥 Give the students 3–5 minutes to discuss the questions in pairs, then quickly elicit ideas from the class. When eliciting ideas, first establish what the placebo effect is, and then encourage brief discussion on questions 2 and 3. Remind the students to support their ideas with examples where possible. Do not feed back in detail at this point, as these questions will be dealt with in the video.

3 ▶ 👤 Students complete the task individually and check their answers in pairs. Quickly elicit the answers from the class.

> **Answers**
> 1 A placebo is a substance which doctors give patients. The patient is told that it is a medicine, although it may actually be something simple with no medical properties at all. The patient may then feel that he or she is getting better, simply because he or she has taken a (fake) medicine. This is called the 'placebo effect'.
> 2 Some people think that placebo medicines can be effective, if the patient really believes that they are medicines.
> 3 Students' own answers.

WHILE WATCHING

UNDERSTANDING MAIN IDEAS

4 ▶ 👤 Students complete the task individually and compare their answers in pairs. Quickly elicit the answers from the class.

> **Answers**
> 1, 3, 4, 6

5 👥 Students discuss the questions in pairs. Quickly elicit the answers from the class.

> **Answers**
> 1 That the brain's ability to recognize pain is flexible.
> 2 Yes.
> 3 The brain can respond to a placebo, and change the amount of pain you feel.

UNDERSTANDING DETAIL

6 ▶ 👤 Students complete the task individually. With a stronger group, you could ask the students to try to answer the questions from memory before checking their answers against the recording.

> **Answers**
> 1 F 2 T 3 F 4 T 5 T 6 T 7 F 8 T

DISCUSSION

7 👥 Give the students up to five minutes to discuss the questions in small groups, then elicit ideas from the class.

LISTENING 1

PREPARING TO LISTEN

UNDERSTANDING KEY VOCABULARY

1 👤 Students complete the task individually and check their answers in pairs. Quickly elicit the answers from the students.

> **Answers**
> 1 f 2 c 3 a 4 i 5 d 6 b 7 h 8 e 9 j 10 g

USING YOUR KNOWLEDGE

2 👥 Students complete the task in pairs. Allow up to five minutes for discussion, then elicit ideas from the class. When discussing question 3, encourage the students to tell you why they think that the people they suggest are geniuses.

3 (◄)) **10.1** 👤 Ask the students to read the options carefully. They should then complete the task individually and check their answers in pairs. You could point out that Dr Anderson might well be a genius, too – but that we don't have that information.

> **Answers**
> 1 b 2 c

WHILE LISTENING

LISTENING FOR MAIN IDEAS

4 (◄)) **10.2** 👤 Ask the students whether they think that the brains of geniuses are different from those of ordinary people. You could also elicit possible answers to questions 3 and 4, but do not comment in detail at this stage. Students complete the task individually and check their answers in pairs.

> **Answers**
> 1 There is no evidence to suggest that geniuses have different brains.
> 2 Being active and doing things can help develop the brain.
> 3 It is a theory that if you spend at least 10,000 hours doing something, then you will be successful at it.
> 4 Working hard: he says genius is 1% inspiration and 99% perspiration.

PRONUNCIATION FOR LISTENING

> **Language note**
>
> Listening for a rising or falling tone at the end of a question can tell us if the speaker is checking information and wants a 'yes/no' answer, or if the speaker is asking for more detailed information.

5 (◀) 10.3) 👤 Ask the students to read the notes on *intonation in questions*. They should then complete the task individually and check their answers in pairs.

> **Answers**
>
> 1 ↗ 2 ↘ 3 ↗ 4 ↘

6 👥 Give the students up to two minutes to discuss their ideas in pairs. You could ask them to practise saying the yes/no questions when answering question 3. Then elicit suggestions from the class. If the students seem unclear about the correct pronunciation of the sentences, play the two dialogues again, stopping after each question so that the students can repeat in chorus.

> **Answers**
>
> 1 1, 3
> 2 2, 4
> 3 rise

7 👥 Give the students time to practise saying the questions out loud. Monitor the class. You could ask students at random to repeat any one particular sentence. Give visual feedback (e.g. a frown for 'incorrect' and a nod for 'correct'), but do not comment in detail.

8 (◀) 10.4) 👤 Students complete the task individually and check their answers in pairs. Quickly elicit the answers from the students.

> **Answers**
>
> 1 falling 2 falling 3 rising 4 rising 5 falling 6 rising

LISTENING FOR DETAIL

9 (◀) 10.2) 👤 Students complete the task individually and check their answers in pairs. Quickly elicit the answers from the students.

> **Answers**
>
> 1 T 2 F 3 T 4 DNS 5 F 6 DNS 7 T 8 F

POST-LISTENING

10 👤👥 Ask the students to read the information box on understanding paraphrase. You could elicit from the class situations in which it might be useful to paraphrase. Students complete the task individually or in pairs. Elicit the answers from the class.

> **Answers**
>
> a determined by our genes
> b determined ... by our environment
> c exceptional
> d if you put 10,000 hours into something

DISCUSSION

11 👥 Students discuss the questions in pairs. Allow 3–5 minutes for discussion, then elicit ideas from the class.

⊙ LANGUAGE DEVELOPMENT

COLLOCATIONS WITH *MIND*

1 👤👥 Students complete the task individually or in pairs. You could do the first question with the class as an example.

> **Answers**
>
> 1 comes to mind 2 make up your mind
> 3 mind your own business 4 speak your mind
> 5 bear/keep in mind 6 Do you mind

2 👥 Students complete the task with a new partner. Set a time limit at the start of the activity of five minutes to discuss the questions in detail (10 minutes with a stronger class). Monitor the class and give feedback at the end. You could elicit some suggestions for the questions that seemed most interesting to your students, or pick up on some of the things you heard while monitoring the students' discussions and use these as the basis of a class discussion.

3 👤👥 Students complete the task individually or in pairs. Elicit the answers from the class.

> **Answers**
>
> 1 Never mind 2 something/anything on your mind
> 3 changed my mind 4 mind what you say

LISTENING 2

PREPARING TO LISTEN

UNDERSTANDING KEY VOCABULARY

1 👤👥 Students complete the task individually or in pairs. Elicit the answers from the class.

> **Answers**
>
> muscles – g
> active – c
> require – b
> decisions – a
> solve – i
> promotes – e
> stimulates – d
> efficiently – f
> beneficial – h

2 👥 Students discuss the sentences in pairs. Allow 2–4 minutes for discussion, then elicit suggested answers from the class. Do not comment in detail at this stage.

3 👤👥 Students complete the task individually or in pairs. Elicit suggestions from the class, but do not comment in detail at this stage.

4 🔊 10.5 👤 Students complete the task individually. Quickly elicit the answers from the students.

> **Answers**
>
> 1 b 2 c

WHILE LISTENING

LISTENING FOR MAIN IDEAS

5 🔊 10.6 👥👤 Ask the students to read the tips and to decide which are the most likely four. Students then check their ideas against the recording. Quickly go through the answers with the class.

> **Answers**
>
> mentioned: 2, 6, 7, 8

LISTENING FOR DETAIL

6 🔊 10.6 👤 Students complete the task individually.

> **Answers**
>
> 1 T 2 DNS 3 T 4 T 5 DNS 6 F 7 F 8 F 9 T

POST-LISTENING

7 👤👥 Students complete the task individually or in pairs. Elicit the answers from the class.

> **Answers**
>
> 2 All in all 3 To sum up 4 In conclusion 5 Finally

8 👤👥 Students answer the question individually or in pairs. Elicit suggestions from the class.

> **Answers**
>
> 1 To make our argument clearer, and remind the listener of our main points.
> 2 It is usually a summary of the main idea or ideas.

DISCUSSION

9 👥 Give the students up to five minutes to discuss the questions in small groups, then elicit ideas from the class.

CRITICAL THINKING

UNDERSTAND

1 👤👥 Ask the students to read the information box on multiple intelligences and to look at the diagram. They should then complete the task individually or in pairs. Quickly elicit the answers from the class, but do not comment too much at this stage. The students will have the chance to explore multiple intelligence theory in more depth in the next tasks.

> **Answers**
>
> 1 c 2 b 3 a 4 e 5 f 6 g 7 d

APPLY

2 👤 Students complete the task individually.

3 👥 Students compare their answers to Exercise 2 with a new partner and then match the actions (a–g) in Exercise 2 with the intelligences in Exercise 1.

> **Suggested answers**
>
> a 1 b 3 c 5 d 4 e 2 f 7 g 6

4 👥 Give the students 4–8 minutes to discuss the intelligences needed for the different occupations. You could ask them to first take brief notes individually and then to use these as the basis of their pair work. Go through the suggested answers for all of the occupations with the class, encouraging further discussion where possible.

EVALUATE

5 👥 Give the students up to 4–8 minutes to discuss the questions in small groups, then elicit ideas from the class. For question 3, you could ask the students to discuss (either with their groups or during a class discussion) the kinds of language tasks that might be best suited to their own intelligences. With a very strong group, you could ask the class to look at one or two pages from one of the units of this book and discuss the different ways that the exercises could be presented to cater for their different intelligences.

SPEAKING

PREPARATION FOR SPEAKING

ASKING FOR ADVICE

1 ◀)) 10.7 👤 👥 Point out that the first question has been done as an example. Students complete the task individually or in pairs. Elicit the answers from the students.

> ### Answers
> 2 what can we do to
> 3 What do you suggest for this
> 4 Do you think we ought to
> 5 What should we do

2 ◀)) 10.7 👤 👥 Students complete the task individually or in pairs. Elicit the answers from the class. If the students seem unclear about the correct intonation of the sentences, play the recording again, stopping after each sentence so that the students can repeat in chorus. You could also call on individual students at random to repeat one or more of the sentences. Remind them to focus on producing the correct rising or falling intonation.

> ### Answers
> 1 ↘ 2 ↘ 3 ↘ 4 ↗ 5 ↘

3 👥 👥👥 Allow 5–8 minutes for the students to complete the task in pairs or small groups. Ask them to discuss the questions in detail, and tell them to be ready to put forward a series of practical suggestions for learners of English at the end of their discussions. Elicit ideas from each group, reminding the groups that they only need make suggestions that have not already been made (or add something to those suggestions).

4 ◀)) 10.8 👤 Ask the students to read the explanation box on modal verbs. Students complete the task individually. Elicit the answers from the class.

> ### Answers
> 2 Make sure that you   3 It would be a good idea to
> 4 It might be good to; make sure 5 You should
> 6 You ought to

5 ◀)) 10.8 👤 👥 Students complete the task individually or in pairs. Elicit the answers from the class. If the students seem unclear about which word is stressed, play the recording again, stopping after each sentence so that the students can repeat in chorus. You could also call on individual students at random to repeat one or more of the sentences. Remind them to focus on stressing the correct word, as well as their pronunciation in general.

6 👥 Give the students three minutes to complete the sentences and write them down in pairs. Ask the students to include a wide variety of activities that accurately reflect their country's culture (both past and present) and history, as well as including visits to well-known areas of natural beauty.

7 👥👥 Students compare their ideas in small groups. You could ask them to come up with a definitive programme. Depending on the class time available, you could ask the groups to think of a set of activities for a person staying 1, 2, 3, 7 or 14 days. Tell the students not to try to cram in too much, and that the visitors will need to take breaks – and will also want to eat! You could also ask them to suggest restaurants and cafés, or to say what kind of food the visitor should sample during their stay.

SPEAKING TASK

PREPARE

1 👤 Ask the students to read the role-play topic and to rank the seven intelligences as they apply to their own learning styles: 1 = most important, 2 = least important. For example, someone who likes to do lots of group work probably has a strong interpersonal intelligence. However, someone with a stronger intrapersonal intelligence would probably prefer to work alone. Give the students 1–2 minutes to complete the ranking, then quickly elicit from each student their strongest and weakest intelligence. You could then suggest ways that you might incorporate this new knowledge into your lesson planning.

2 👤 Ask the students to stay in the same pairs and to each choose a role. Give them three minutes to take notes on their roles individually.

3 👥 Students complete the task in pairs. Allow 2–4 minutes for the discussion.

PRACTISE

4 👥 Set a time limit of five minutes for the students to practise their role-play in pairs.

5 👥 Set a time limit of five minutes for the students to complete the task in pairs. When the students have finished, quickly elicit summaries and/or suggestions from the groups. You could ask them to focus on ideas that have not already been discussed with the class.

TASK CHECKLIST AND OBJECTIVES REVIEW

Refer students to the end of each unit for the Task checklist and Objectives review. Students complete the tables individually to reflect on their learning and identify areas for improvement.

WORDLIST

See Training tips, pages 9–11 for ideas about how to make the most of the Wordlist with your students.

REVIEW TEST

See pages 116–117 for the photocopiable Review test for this unit, and page 91 for ideas about when and how to administer the Review test.

ADDITIONAL SPEAKING TASK

See page 127 for an Additional speaking task related to this unit.

Put students in groups of three. Focus students on the discussion topics in the box. Ask students to choose two topics each. Give them two minutes to make notes on their topics. Then, students take turns to speak about one of their topics for between one and two minutes. The other students listen and ask questions at the end to find out more about what advice the speaker would give on the topic. They can also give their own opinion on the topic. This continues until all students have spoken about their two topics.

RESEARCH PROJECT

Create a video about a famous genius.

Divide your class into groups and explain that each group will be responsible for creating a video explaining the life of a genius, e.g. Albert Einstein, Galileo Galilei, Leonardo da Vinci, Johann Wolfgang von Goethe, Ludwig van Beethoven, Stephen Hawkins, Marie Curie, Émilie du Châtelet. Students could find out what was special about these people and why they are considered geniuses.

Each group will use their research to create a video to present to children. Students will first need to create a script or storyboard. They will also have to think about who in the group will work the camera, who will direct the video, who will edit it, and who will present or narrate the information. The videos could then be uploaded to a video-sharing website and promoted to local schools.

REVIEW TESTS ANSWERS AND AUDIO SCRIPTS

The *Review tests* are designed to be used after the students have completed each unit of the Student's book. Each *Review test* checks students' knowledge of the key language areas and practices the listening skills from the unit. The *Review tests* take around 50 minutes to complete but you may wish to adjust this time depending on your class or how much of the Student's book unit you covered.

Review tests can be given as homework as general revision. *Review test* audio is accessed from the Cambridge LMS. Use the *Additional speaking tasks* at the end of the Teacher's Book or in the Online Workbook to test your students' speaking skills. Photocopy one test for each student. Students should do the tests on their own. You can check the answers by giving students their peers' papers to mark or correct the papers yourself. Keep a record of the results to help monitor individual student progress.

REVIEW TEST 1 ANSWERS

1 1 con<u>v</u>inced 2 relo<u>c</u>ated 3 sur<u>v</u>ive
4 comm<u>u</u>nicate 5 <u>p</u>oisonous 6 <u>h</u>armless 7 en<u>v</u>ironment
8 <u>t</u>reated 9 <u>r</u>ealize 10 con<u>d</u>itions
2 1 F 2 F 3 F 4 T 5 T 6 F 7 F 8 F 9 T 10 T
3 1 analysis 2 environmental 3 communication
4 involvement 5 abuse
4 1 involved 2 abuse 3 analysis 4 environmental
5 communication
5 1 T 2 F 3 F 4 T 5 F

REVIEW TEST 1 AUDIO SCRIPTS

🔊 **1.1**

1	con<u>v</u>inced	5	<u>p</u>oisonous	9	<u>r</u>ealize
2	relo<u>c</u>ated	6	<u>h</u>armless	10	con<u>d</u>itions
3	sur<u>v</u>ive	7	en<u>v</u>ironment		
4	comm<u>u</u>nicate	8	<u>t</u>reated		

🔊 **1.2**

It's not that I don't like dogs, more that I don't really have any strong feelings about them. Many people say that you're either a cat person or a dog person. I'm neither. I guess you could say that I'm a people person. I'm certainly not an animal person. They're OK, but I'd never spend the day at the zoo – not when there are so many other things to do. I went as a kid, but not now. People say that having animals brings all kinds of benefits, but I'm not convinced. I guess I'm the wrong person to ask about animals. We did have a dog when I was a child, his name was Buster. But we relocated to America for a year and left it with our neighbours, who took care of it. I'm sorry to say that I didn't really think about him while I was away. Anyway, it became ill and died shortly after we returned. Actually, I did feel upset about that. I remember when we came back from America – the dog was so happy to see me. He remembered me – maybe he even missed me. He was running around the house, so excited when he saw me after a year. Maybe that was his way of communicating with me. I really enjoyed playing with him, and taking him to run in the park. But after Buster

died, my parents asked if we should get another dog. I said no. At that time, I was becoming more interested in playing with friends, or even playing on my computer. Buster was the last pet I ever had. I don't think it was an especially sad experience, but I can't imagine getting another pet. Maybe if my son wants one when he's older, but so far he's not shown any interest in animals. If we did ever get a pet, I'd like to think we'd find an abandoned cat or puppy. I'm certainly not into exotic animals – certainly nothing poisonous, or too far removed from its natural environment like a snake or a reptile. Something fairly harmless, like a cat or a rabbit or something similar. There are already enough badly treated animals around without us encouraging pet shops to breed more. I realize that an animal raised in poor conditions might be more difficult to look after. But if we ever do get another pet, I'd like it to be one that really does need a new home.

REVIEW TEST 2 ANSWERS

1 1 Wha<u>t</u> was so good abou<u>t</u> Austria?
2 There are grea<u>t</u> summers, and spring is jus<u>t</u> amazing.
3 Was i<u>t</u> a festival or was i<u>t</u> something else?
4 Wha<u>t</u> happens in this festival – wha<u>t</u> are the people doing?
5 People wear a lo<u>t</u> of different things.
2 1 F 2 F 3 T 4 T 5 F 6 T 7 F 8 F 9 F 10 F
3 1 identity 2 generations 3 alive 4 traditional 5 behaviour
4 1 useless 2 traditional 3 careful 4 enjoyable 5 celebration
5 1 social 2 throughout 3 anniversary 4 affect 5 global
6 1 T 2 F 3 T 4 T 5 F

REVIEW TEST 2 AUDIO SCRIPTS

🔊 **2.1**

1 What was so good about Austria?
2 There are great summers, and spring is just amazing.
3 Was it a festival or was it something else?
4 What happens in this festival – what are the people doing?
5 People wear a lot of different things.

🔊 **2.2**

A: So, tell me about your time in Austria. How was it?
B: It was great. Really nice. I really enjoyed working there. I'd love to go back one day. But, you know, it's great to come back to London, too!
A: What was so good about Austria? I've never been there.
B: Well lots of things. The weather's wonderful. There are great summers, and spring is just amazing. It's hot, but you can always go walking in the mountains. And autumn and winter are nice too. They are cool, but it snows, and you can go skiing everywhere. There is always something to do. Did you look at any of the photos I sent you?
A: Yes, some of them. The countryside looks fantastic. And I saw some photos with lots of people wearing crazy masks. Was it a festival or was it something else?
B: Oh yes, that was the *Mullerlaufen*. Yes, it's a traditional festival, or carnival. It happens every four years, so I was really lucky to see it. And it takes place in the Martha villages, in the countryside.
A: The *Muller* – what? The Martha villages? What are they?
B: It's a name given to five villages in the eastern part of Austria. The first letter of each village spells the word *Martha*.
A: Oh, right. M-A-R-T … hang on, there are six letters in *Martha*.

B: OK, well, one of the villages is a place called Thaur, with a 'TH'. And I was working in Rum.

A: You were working in a room?

B: No, Rum. That's the name of a village – the 'R' village.

A: Oh, I see. Sorry, this is complicated!

B: Anyway, the masks are worn by the *Mullers*.

A: The Mullers. So they're a family, right?

B: No, no. The Mullers represent the four seasons. They each wear wooden masks. Spring is the youngest, then summer, autumn and finally winter. And they all have different characters, and look and behave in different ways.

A: It sounds interesting. So what happens in this festival – what are the people doing?

B: Well, it's really more like a carnival – because the people are on the streets wearing special clothes, and there is special food and dancing.

A: And everyone takes part?

B: Oh sure, yes. Old and young – everyone in the family comes out and enjoys themselves!

A: That's good. It's good when traditions can be kept alive, and not left to die out.

B: Yes. In the smaller villages, the dress tends to be very traditional. Each village expresses its own identity through the costumes they wear.

A: What are the costumes made of?

B: Well, some are very simple, but some are very complicated – with jewels and pearls. And in the larger towns, it's more like Halloween in America. People wear a **lot** of different things in this festival.

A: You mean, like ghosts and monsters?

B: Well, no … I meant that, in America, people wear lots of different things at Halloween – like superhero costumes or … you can even see people dressed as food, like hamburgers or pizza! I mean that in this Austrian festival, *Mullerlaufen*, people wear lots of different kinds of clothes. Anything, really. It's all very colourful.

A: So did you dress up?

B: Me? No. This festival is more for the villagers, really, and the tourists can interact, but don't get dressed up. I just watched and took lots of photos!

A: OK, I think I'll need to check your blog again!

REVIEW TEST 3 ANSWERS

1 1 We've got **to** give **a** presentation about **a** person **from** history.
2 Plato said **that** she **was** one **of the** greatest poets he **had** read.
3 She **was a** British women's rights activist who lived in **the** late 1900s.
4 **Have** you heard **of** her?
5 **That was the** start **of the** equal rights movement in America.

2 1 F 2 T 3 F 4 F 5 F 6 T 7 T 8 T 9 F 10 T

3 1 rulers 2 ancient 3 significant 4 period 5 exchange

4 1 which 2 where 3 who 4 where 5 which

5 1 She ~~found~~ discovered the treasure while digging in her garden.
2 He sent his ~~warriors~~ soldiers across Europe, conquering every country in their path.
3 At the time of his death, he was the oldest ~~emperor~~ ruler the world had ever known.
4 There are ~~plenty~~ lots of books there to keep you busy. You should be able to find everything you need.
5 So just how many of these ~~old~~ ancient statues are there on the island?

6 1 decade 2 late 3 medieval 4 at the age 5 at that time

REVIEW TEST 3 AUDIO SCRIPTS

🔊 **3.1**

1 We've got to give a presentation about a person from history.
2 Plato said that she was one of the greatest poets he had read.
3 She was a British women's rights activist who lived in the late 1900s.
4 Have you heard of her?
5 That was the start of the equal rights movement in America.

🔊 **3.2**

Gemma: OK. So we've got to give **a** presentation about **a** person from history. What do you think, Susan?

Susan: I'm really not sure. What do you think, Gemma? Do you think it has to be a famous person?

Gemma: Well, no, it should be someone who we can find lots of information about. Someone interesting who is worth giving a presentation about!

Susan: Yes. And I thought it'd be better if we chose someone less well known. Not someone who everyone knows. Then our presentation will be more interesting, I think. That way, maybe someone might actually learn something for once!

Gemma: So who did you have in mind?

Susan: I was thinking about women in history. History is very often about men, you know.

Gemma: Is it?

Susan: I'm afraid it is. A lot of famous writers, politicians, rulers – all men. But there were women in history, too!

Gemma: Well, yes, of course there were!

Susan: So, how about Sappho?

Gemma: I've never heard of … her? Was Sappho a woman?

Susan: She was, yes. She was a very important woman.

Gemma: Was she a politician?

Susan: Actually, one of the first published female writers.

Gemma: Oh really? And what did she write? When was she published? Two hundred years ago?

Susan: No! She was writing more than 2,000 years ago! And she was a poet, and she lived in ancient Greece.

Gemma: Oh, I see.

Susan: I think that Plato said that she was one of the greatest poets he **had** read.

Gemma: Hmm. OK, but there have been lots more poets since Plato's time. Anyway, I'm not sure I'm interested in poetry. Any other ideas? Anyone more modern?

Susan: Emmeline Pankhurst?

Gemma: Was she a poet?

Susan: No, she **was a** British women's rights activist who lived in **the** late 1900s. When she was alive, women in the UK couldn't vote in elections. But she worked and worked. And in the end, the British government gave women the same voting rights as men. Unfortunately, although she had a major, significant effect on British life, she died just before women got the vote.

Gemma: Interesting. That reminds me of Rosa Parks. **Have** you heard **of** her?

Susan: I think so, yes. Wasn't she a Black woman living in America?

Gemma: Yes, that's right. She lived some time after Emmeline Pankhurst. Actually, it was in the 1950s that she became famous.

Susan: Oh yes. And at that period, actually, in 1955, to be exact, Black Americans didn't have equal rights. They had to go to different schools …

Gemma: Yes, and they even had different seats on the buses and trains.

Susan: So what did Rosa Parks do?

Gemma: Well, she went on a bus – and she wasn't a young woman, she was in her 40s – and she sat in the seats reserved for Black people – at the back of the bus. Then the bus got full up. And a White man came on and asked Rosa to give him her seat.

Susan: And what happened?

Gemma: Well, she said no! And everyone was shocked – because, of course, a Black person should always give up their seat on a bus to a White person.

Susan: And then?

Gemma: Everyone was shocked, and she was arrested!

Susan: Really?

Gemma: And when the news spread, this made people aware of the real differences between Black and White people, and that actually, life was unfair.

Susan: And **that was the** start **of the** equal rights movement in America. All started by one ordinary woman who only wanted to sit on a bus!

Gemma: That's right.

Susan: OK. So why don't we talk about two people – Emmeline Pankhurst and Rosa Parks. Two ordinary women who changed their countries.

Gemma: Good idea. You research Emmeline Pankhurst, and I'll research Rosa Parks. Then we can get together tomorrow, and exchange information.

Susan: Great!

REVIEW TEST 4 ANSWERS

1 1c 2b 3b 4b 5c
2 1 F 2 F 3 T 4 F 5 T 6 T 7 F 8 T 9 T 10 F
3 1 research 2 present 3 increase 4 decrease 5 control
4 1 slower 2 better 3 more interesting 4 the most comfortable 5 easier
5 1 relax 2 injured 3 challenges 4 damaged 5 goals
6 1 attitudes 2 convenience 3 achieved 4 fuel 5 turbulence

REVIEW TEST 4 AUDIO SCRIPTS

◀)) 4.1

A: Hi. Taking a break?

B: Yes. I'm seriously in need of coffee.

A: Great. I'll join you. It's a bit lonely in our office today.

B: Actually, do you mind if I take a quick look at your paper?

A: Sure. I hope you don't need the features section, I tore an article out before coming to work. I want to show it to my wife.

B: Oh, right. What was it about?

A: It was a report. Some people did research into accidents involving children who text while walking. They're really shocking.

B: Yes. I think it would be safer if children didn't text all the time. They're always glued to their phones. They can't concentrate on what's around them.

A: Well, yes. That would be safer. But it's not going to happen. Anyway, we all text – not just kids. In my opinion, we should all be more careful.

B: Maybe, but it's not really enough just to say 'we should all be more careful'. Someone has to do something!

A: Like what?

B: Like make it impossible to text while walking.

A: What? How?

B: Well, I don't know! Maybe they could build a safety feature into the design of the phone. So it doesn't work if it's moving.

A: That's not a safety feature – that's a broken phone! No one would buy a mobile phone you couldn't use while walking. It wouldn't be mobile!

B: Or they could include some safety features that parents could turn on if they wanted.

A: Oh, come on. Most kids would work out how to change the settings in under two seconds!

B: OK. But I've seen kids walking out into the road on the way to school and nearly being hit by cars. I'm worried that one day my kids will cause a crash. Or worse …

A: I read that road accidents involving children double at 11.

B: Really? My children are that age.

A: Hmm.

B: So why the increase in accidents?

A: Because it's around that age that children get their first mobiles. Their friends all have them, so they want one, too.

B: That's actually got me worried. I bought my kids mobiles as a present for their birthdays so I could keep in touch with them. I thought they'd be safer. Now I'm not so sure.

A: I think it would be much better if drivers were more careful when driving through busy areas. They should look out for kids, you can't expect them be sensible all the time. They should teach this when you learn to drive.

B: Well, we can't ban using a mobile phone while walking.

A: No, it's not a crime.

B: But we need to decrease the number of accidents. More effort should be made to educate kids in the proper use of mobile phones. Maybe at school?

A: So again, teachers have to work harder? Schools can't control what the kids are doing in their own free time – that's down to the parents.

B: I disagree. Schools should always try to teach kids about the dangers they face outside school hours.

A: Hmm. Well, parents should also do this, too. Anyway, I need to talk to my wife about this when I get home tonight …

◀)) 4.2

1 Some people did research into accidents involving children who text while walking.
2 I bought my kids mobiles as a present for their birthdays so I could keep in touch with them.
3 Why the increase in accidents?
4 We need to decrease the number of accidents.
5 Schools can't control what the kids are doing in their own free time – that's down to the parents.

REVIEW TEST 5 ANSWERS

1 1 T 2 F 3 F 4 T 5 F 6 F 7 T 8 F
2 1 greenhouse 2 irresponsible 3 long-term 4 disagreement 5 extreme 6 diseases 7 climate 8 fuels
3 1 /w/ 2 /r/ 3 /w/ 4 /r/
4 1 ir 2 anti 3 in 4 im 5 mis
5 1 might 2 will 3 can't 4 may 5 could
6 1 disaster 2 disadvantage 3 drawback 4 benefits 5 affordable

REVIEW TEST 5 AUDIO SCRIPTS

◀)) 5.1

Presenter: And just to remind the listeners at home, you can now join the debate by calling the usual number. And I think we have our first caller. Yes, it's a Mrs Trellis, from Wales. What do you want to say on the subject of climate change, Mrs Trellis?

Mrs Trellis: Well, I'm not sure that climate change is a bad thing, is it? I heard that temperatures might go up because of greenhouse gases. Why is that bad? Everyone likes warmer weather, don't they? I would love to have warm, sunny winters!

Presenter: Well, that's rather an irresponsible attitude, Mrs Trellis. Most experts think that even a small increase in temperature could have catastrophic long-term effects. And of course, climate change doesn't only mean that the temperature will be warmer. It might be colder, or it might be wetter. There will be more hurricanes, more floods, in some countries. And I don't think anyone likes hurricanes! Our next caller … We have Robert Shaw on the line. Robert, I understand that **you're involved** in climate research?

Robert: Yes, that's right. The point I wanted to make … I think that these scientific experts … They often disagree about climate change, don't they? Everyone always has a different opinion.

Presenter: So, you're saying that not all scientists agree that climate change is happening?

Robert: Well, most do agree that it is happening. But there is a lot of disagreement as to whether or not it's a bad thing. The debate **too often** centres around areas of extreme climate, like in Africa. Or tiny islands that will be under water in a few hundred years time. Few people talk about how it will affect most of the world. Like Europe. Or North America.

Presenter: Well, **America and Europe** are just two continents, and it does seem clear that climate change could have catastrophic effects across the globe. As I said to Mrs Trellis, hurricanes and floods are becoming more common in the US. Take New York for example, if you remember Hurricane Katrina or Hurricane Sandy. Next, we have a Ms Tyler on the line. Ms Tyler, what was your comment?

Ms Tyler: Hello. Yes. Well, I'm worried about climate change.

Presenter: OK. And why is that?

Ms Tyler: Well … the way we abuse the planet is unnatural. And now the planet is fighting back. We don't know for sure, but my understanding is that a warmer planet may lead to new diseases.

Presenter: That is possible. For example, insects like mosquitoes might move to other countries if the temperature is warmer everywhere.

Ms Tyler: Yes. Malaria, for example, is one disease which might become more common. And what about plants? If the climate changes, will plants be able to survive? Will we have enough to eat or drink? We need to do more research.

Presenter: Thank you. We've time for one last email before the news. And it's Saffron from London. Hello, she writes. I'm 12 and I think that climate change is definitely happening. Some of your callers sound very selfish. It's stupid to say that we'll be happier with a warmer climate. It's not just us, it's the whole world. All the presidents and queens and prime ministers should just get together, make things better, and ban fossil fuels. But they never will. And now over to the news desk.

🔊 5.2

1 I heard that temperatures might go up because of greenhouse gases.
2 But there is a lot of disagreement as to whether or not it's a bad thing.
3 The debate too often centres around areas of extreme climate, like in Africa.
4 Malaria, for example, is one disease which might become more common.

REVIEW TEST 6 ANSWERS

1 1 a 2 a 3 b 4 a 5 b 6 c 7 b 8 a 9 a 10 c
2 1 T 2 F 3 T 4 F 5 F 6 T 7 F 8 T 9 T 10 T
3 1 out 2 up 3 on 4 up 5 over 6 up 7 out 8 up 9 down 10 over
4 1 regularly 2 habit 3 ingredients 4 natural 5 overweight

REVIEW TEST 6 AUDIO SCRIPTS

🔊 6.1

Lauren: Hi Mark! I haven't seen you in ages!

Mark: Oh hi Lauren. I know. Mum says we should meet, but … we never have time.

Lauren: So, how's it going? Mum said you were going to the gym now, is that true?

Mark: Yes, I was talking to mum last week …Mum is wrong, but I did buy a crosstrainer a while ago, and I'm actually using it at home!

Lauren: A crosstrainer? Is that one of those running machines?

Mark: Not really running. I don't like running. It's more a kind of walking. It gives your body an all-round workout. It's good for everything.

Lauren: I can see that! You must have lost about 5 kilos since I last saw you!

Mark: I've actually lost about 8 kilos of fat and put on three kilos of muscle.

Lauren: Wow. That's great! So, what brought this on?

Mark: I caught myself in the mirror in a shop a few months ago. I thought, hey – that fat person looks like me. Then I realized it was me!

Lauren: Oh dear. But you were never that fat, really.

Mark: Thanks, but I was quite overweight. It just kind of happens, slowly. You get into bad habits.

Lauren: Tell me about it! I've not had any regular exercise since the kids were born. I sometimes go out for walks, but it's not the same as the daily runs I used to have.

Mark: So you've given up running?

Lauren: Not given up. My life is just too busy. I really hope I can go running again soon. Weren't you really fit a few years ago?

Mark: A few? That must have been about 15 years ago now, when I first met my wife … I felt great. I was doing lots of sport, eating healthily. I had lots more free time then – and used to do loads of swimming and skiing.

Lauren: And then you got an office job!

Mark: Hah! Yes, lots of sitting in front of a computer.

Lauren: So anyway, why the new healthy lifestyle? Is it a new dad thing?

Mark: Possibly, yes. I really do want to get back into shape, but yes – I also want to be fit for Ben. It'll be great when we can go swimming and hiking together. And I want to be in shape by the time that happens!

Lauren: It looks as though that won't be a problem! How much time are you spending on this thing? The cross trainer?

Mark: Every day. About an hour. Sometimes a little more if Ben sleeps in.

Lauren: So you look after him in the morning? Still no nanny, then?

Mark: No. I love spending that time with my son. Anyway, I usually do 15–30 minutes when I wake up, then a quick shower. When Ben's in bed, I do about 45 minutes in front of the TV.

Lauren: So you work out in front of the TV?

Mark: Yeah. Otherwise it'd be boring. I'd like to go to a gym, but they are too expensive. And I don't want to go to a place with lots of really fit people. I would feel bad.

Lauren: Right. Well, it's nice to see that you've found a way to get healthy!

Mark: Yeah. I want to get down to about 75 kilos. Only another 20 kilos to go!

Lauren: Well, next time I come to your house, I'll take a look. Maybe I'll borrow it from you!

Mark: Sorry, I'm not giving it away! I need to exercise every day … I want to stay healthy!

REVIEW TEST 7 ANSWERS

1 1 T 2 F 3 T 4 T 5 F 6 F 7 T 8 F 9 T 10 T
2 1 a 2 a 3 b 4 c 5 c
3 1 Y 2 N 3 N 4 N 5 Y
4 1 mistake 2 difference 3 discovery 4 mind 5 sure
5 1 were discovered 2 was invented 3 developed 4 was sent
   5 designed
6 1 T 2 F 3 F 4 T 5 F

REVIEW TEST 7 AUDIO SCRIPTS

🔊 7.1

Ruth: Hello. A few shows ago we invited our listeners to go to our Facebook page and post stories of old electronic gadgets they just couldn't bear to throw away.

Alan: That's right. And what a response we had! It seems that many of you have attics full of aging laptops and games consoles dating back to the 1980s. So do go to our Facebook page and have a look at the stories and pictures we've been getting. There really are some great tales.

Ruth: Yes, there certainly are. And one of them in particular caught our eye.

Alan: We've invited Jeannie Cordeaux along to tell us about her much-loved device. Jeannie welcome to the show. Or should I say: welcome to the show.

Jeannie: Thanks!

Ruth: Yes. Listeners may have picked up on that clue. Because Jeannie has come in today to tell us about her favourite toy, her 'Speak & Spell'.

Alan: Listeners younger than us may not know what a Speak & Spell is.

Ruth: Or was.

Alan: Jeannie, can you tell us something about it, please?

Jeannie: Of course. The Speak & Spell toys were very popular throughout the 1980s. In fact, they were produced right up until 1992. I've got an original from when it was first launched in 1978. They'd actually developed a more sophisticated model by the time I bought mine, but the great thing about the first edition is …

Ruth: That's right. Jeannie's model looks like a flat orange box with a handle at the top … it's about 20 by 25 cm, with a small green screen and a yellow keyboard. There are several educational games included, each of them designed to teach spelling.

Alan: And when did you get yours?

Jeannie: I got mine for my birthday, 1982. It was second hand, but in good condition.

Alan: And it was designed to teach children to spell. How did it achieve that?

Jeannie: By saying words out loud in a voice not far from the one you used when you introduced me.

Alan: Spell 'friends. Spell 'decision'. Spell 'appointment'.

Jeannie: Exactly. But I don't think that the words were as difficult as that.

Ruth: Right, so it was really just a toy.

Jeannie: Yes. And I used to like typing in my name and getting it to say 'Hello Jeannie'!

Ruth: Right. … and of course, the Speak & Spell was featured in a recent movie?

Jeannie: Yes. It was in the *Toy Story* films. It's a character called 'Mr Spell'.

Ruth: Right yes, I think I've seen that! So Jeannie, I suppose that your spelling must be excellent now, is that right?

Jeannie: Hah! Maybe! But, you know, it was only a toy, so the words were quite simple. And sometimes, I couldn't always understand the instructions because it had an American accent. So my machine would say 'bath' and I would spell 'bath' with two As because of the way it sounded. And of course, sometimes the American spelling is different from the British spelling – colour for example is spelled C-O-L-O-U-R in British English. But in American English there is no U. So, I'm afraid I often got the answers wrong! But, actually, when I became older, I loved words, and reading, and now my spelling is quite good. So maybe my toy helped after all!

Alan: Now of course, children would have a mobile phone app, or a computer game to play this kind of game.

Jeannie: Yes, and that's fine. I do believe that anything that helps you practise your spelling when you are young is great, in my opinion.

Ruth: Jeannie, thanks very much for coming along to *This Morning.*

Jeannie: It's a pleasure.

🔊 7.2

1 Yes, there certainly are.
2 The Speak & Spell toys were very popular throughout the 1980s.
3 It was designed to teach children to spell.
4 So it was really just a toy.
5 I do believe that anything that helps you practise your spelling when you are young is great.

REVIEW TEST 8 ANSWERS

1 1 F 2 T 3 F 4 T 5 T 6 F 7 F
2 1 b 2 c 3 c 4 b 5 c 6 b 7 a 8 b
3 1 fashionable 2 cameras 3 different 4 unfortunately
   5 interesting
4 1 that 2 concerned 3 mad 4 hand 5 fun
5 1 it's going to rain 2 arrives 3 are having 4 I'll 5 I'll drive
6 1 What do you think 2 How do you feel about 3 Don't you
   agree 4 Do you mean that 5 I see what you mean

REVIEW TEST 8 AUDIO SCRIPTS

🔊 8.1

A: Go to any high street and you'll see people wearing everything from the cheapest lycra tops to the most expensive fabrics. But this year, you're 17.8% less likely to see fashionable clothing than last year. That's according to a new survey published this week. And with me is the woman who did the research, Judy Hubbard. Judy, you say we're now 17.8% less fashionable. How did you come to such a precise figure?

B: Well, it sounds odd, but it *is* the result of information collected from photos we took with our own cameras, photos posted on social networking sites, interviews in the streets and articles we got from magazines.

A: OK. And when did this research begin?

B: We started to collect data from our readers two years ago following a debate on the letters page of *Looks!* magazine. We wanted to know whether or not there really was a general trend away from what might be described as *fashionable* clothing towards cheaper, less attractive designs.

A: And what did your readers think?

B: Well, although our readers *all* stated that they were careful to keep up with fashion, most thought that other people cared much less about fashion two years ago than they did just a few years earlier. They were either earning less, saving more or simply spending their money on things other than clothes.

A: I see. So you started checking the data to see whether the views expressed by your readers were correct?

B: That's right. Last year, using all the information available to us, we tried to get an accurate picture about how fashionable Britain was two years ago.

A: And how fashionable were we back then?

B: On a scale of 100, we stood at about 23.

A: 23? That doesn't sound very good.

B: Actually, it's rather better than we were expecting.

A: And how does that compare to other European countries?

B: Unfortunately, we don't have any data for Europe. But the US edition of *Looks!* carried out similar research, and America was slightly ahead of us with a score of 27.

A: Right. Still not that great. How do things stand now?

B: Well, as you pointed out earlier, we were 17.8% less fashionable last year than two years ago. But, the US was about 2% more fashionable.

A: So, a small increase for the US but a rather dramatic fall for us. Why?

B: It's difficult to say, but there do seem to be a number of factors. The main one being lifestyle choices.

A: Lifestyle choices? What do you mean by that?

B: Well, while it *is* true that most people have less money to spend, that doesn't really account for the general trend away from fashionable clothing.

A: Right. So how *do* you account for the decline?

B: Well, it seems that people are getting fatter in the UK. In the 1980s and 90s, many British people were happy to disguise their size by wearing fashionable sportswear.

A: So why are things different?

B: Basically, we've got so big that it's now very difficult to find nice clothes that fit us. Many people think there's no point going to any of the better clothes stores, because there's nothing for them to buy. And fashion companies don't want to make clothes for very fat people.

A: Because it's not great for their image?

B: That's right. They're now focusing more on the kinds of things you might see in music videos. So there's a definite gap in the market, and no one seems to have stepped in. And as a result, it's getting more difficult for the larger person to dress with confidence. And unfortunately, the general trend is towards a fatter, less fashionable Britain.

A: And what are your predictions for next year?

B: Well, I don't think people are going to get thinner, unfortunately. I don't know the future, but perhaps Britain will become more unfashionable.

A: Well, that's certainly an interesting point of view. Judy Hubbard, thank you. Back to the studio …

🔊 **8.2**

1 This year, you're 17.8% less likely to see fashionable clothing than last year.
2 It *is* the result of information collected from photos we took with our own cameras …
3 So why are things different?
4 I don't think people are going to get thinner, unfortunately.
5 Well, that's certainly an interesting point of view.

REVIEW TEST 9 ANSWERS

1 1 c 2 c 3 b 4 a 5 b
2 1 F 2 T 3 T 4 T 5 F 6 T 7 F 8 T 9 F 10 T
3 1 answer 2 surprising 3 exactly 4 debts 5 doubt
4 1 credit card 2 cash 3 lend 4 bill
5 1 save 2 paid 3 save 4 pays 5 lent 6 paid
6 1 d 2 a 3 e 4 b 5 c

REVIEW TEST 9 AUDIO SCRIPTS

🔊 **9.1**

Researcher: Excuse me, would you mind answering a few questions about money and spending?

Interviewee: Er … OK, I'm in a bit of a hurry – actually, I need to catch a train soon.

Researcher: It's OK, I won't take long. I just have a few questions.

Interviewee: Well, OK. I hope I can answer them, but I need to go in five minutes. Otherwise, I'll miss my train!

Researcher: Thank you so much for your time. I'm carrying out some research into the money people spend on travelling to and from work.

Interviewee: Right, OK. Sure. That's a good question actually. The train prices went up a lot this year. And it was surprising, because I don't think the quality of the service went up. It's not something I'm very happy about …

Researcher: No, of course. Can I ask which income bracket you fall into? Up to £10,000 a year, £10–25,000, £25–50,000, £50–75,000 or over £75,000?

Interviewee: Well, I think … £25–50,000.

Researcher: Great, thanks. And how often do you use public transport? Never, 1–2 times a week, 3 times a week, 4–5 times a week or every day?

Interviewee: Well, I use the train every day. Every week day, that is. I don't go anywhere on the weekend, or I use the car.

Researcher: So that's about 5 times a week.

Interviewee: I think so, yes. Usually.

Researcher: Thanks. How important would you say public transport is to you? Extremely important, very important, quite important, not very important or really not very important at all?

Interviewee: Well, it's really very important, of course.

Researcher: Can you explain why?

Interviewer: Why? Well, otherwise, I wouldn't be able to get to work.

Researcher: Right. I'll put you down for extremely important, then.

Interviewee: Sorry, will this take long? I think I need to run to my train now …

Researcher: Just a few more questions! And what sort of public transport do you use regularly?

Interviewee: Well, trains, obviously, as I've just said.

Researcher: OK, yes, sorry, you've already said that.

Interviewee: Do you have a lot more questions?

Researcher: Just a couple more. Could I just ask you generally how much value for money is represented by public transport?

Interviewee: Well … the trains are very expensive, and they are often late, and crowded. And, you know, I have to pay over £4,000 a year commuting to and from work, and that's a lot of money. Unfortunately, I don't have a choice. Because if I drove to work, if I took my car, then I'd be stuck in a traffic jam for hours, and of course, the petrol is getting more and more expensive these days, too.

Researcher: And how much of your income is taken up by commuting?

Interviewee: I don't know exactly. Quite a lot. It's about 10%. And I think that's too much.

Reviewer: Can you explain why you think it's too much?

Interviewee: Well, it wouldn't be so bad if I was guaranteed a seat on the train, but I'm not. I usually have to stand. I earn more than many people, but I'm not especially wealthy. And I can't afford to pay for a seat reservation. I certainly can't afford to travel first class. Look, I use the train to go to work because I have to. I go to work to pay the bills. I earn a reasonable income, and have relatively few debts. It costs me a lot of money to travel to work, it really does. Our public transport system is overcrowded and overpriced. It's always been like that, and I doubt that it will change in the near future.

Researcher: Er, thank you. Could I…

Interviewee: Look, I'm sorry – but I don't really have any more time. My train is here soon!

Researcher: OK. Well, thanks for your time.

Interviewee: That's fine. Bye.

🔊 **9.2**

1 I hope I can answer them, but I need to go in five minutes.
2 And it was surprising, because I don't think the quality of the service went up.
3 **Researcher:** And how much of your income is taken up by commuting?
   Interviewee: I don't know exactly.
4 I earn a reasonable income, and have relatively few debts.
5 It's always been like that, and I doubt that it will change in the near future.

REVIEW TEST 10 ANSWERS

1 1 T 2 T 3 F 4 F 5 T 6 F 7 T 8 F 9 T 10 T
2 1 change your mind 2 unique 3 talented 4 respond 5 exceptional
3 1 ↑ 2 ↓ 3 ↓ 4 ↓ 5 ↑
4 1 changed 2 business 3 Never 4 have 5 make 6 bear/keep 7 would 8 speak
5 1 occurred 2 intelligent 3 theory 4 ordinary 5 efficiently 6 determine 7 experiments

REVIEW TEST 10 AUDIO SCRIPTS

🔊 **10.1**

Hello, and thank you all for downloading this week's podcast with news and views of all the latest games.

So, let's start with a difficult question. Are computer games bad for us? Especially for children? Many people think that computer games are a waste of time, and don't teach you everything. Well, that might be true. But, luckily, not all computer games are the same. One software company has asked the question: What can we do to make computer games more intelligent? How can computer games keep our brains healthy and active? And they have created a new game called *Annie Pond and the Box of Time*. We think it will change your mind about computer games. This is our review.

Annie Pond and the Box of Time is unique. It's different from the usual action-adventure games that many people play, or simple strategy games like Angry Birds. This game features realistic characters, and different puzzles which really train your brain.

So, what happens in this game? Well, firstly, *Annie Pond and the Box of Time*, gives hours and hours of entertainment. You can play it at any time – on your computer, or on your phone – at home, or on the train or bus. And it has a very interesting story which keeps you interested for weeks and weeks.

The main character, Annie Pond, is an extremely talented teenage detective who spends her time solving mysteries. You play Annie Pond, and you are having a boring day, when you suddenly receive an unexpected email. However, this email is very strange. There is no information about who sent the message, and it seems to come from the future. No, not the year 3000, the next century or even next year. According to the date on the email, it was posted next *week*. The email contains just one sentence: *Don't go to school tomorrow, Annie Pond!* What does it all mean? Annie Pond immediately tries to work out what's going on. The game then takes you all around the world – from Scotland to New Zealand – to solve the mystery. You meet strange and wonderful characters, and and soon find yourself in dangerous and exciting situations.

Overall, in this game, you have to solve about 200 puzzles to unravel the mystery. The puzzles vary in difficulty: as the game continues, the puzzles get more difficult.

Now, we're not going to tell you what the mystery is, because we don't want to say too much. And luckily, this is one game where you can't solve all the mysteries easily in one go.

The game is a lot of fun if you don't usually like traditional puzzles. The game has different activities for different types of intelligences. It has puzzles which test your logical intelligence, puzzles which test your musical intelligence, linguistic intelligence, and so on. While this may sound annoying, it does make the game very interesting. You need to respond to the game, and change the way you think. This gives you good brain training.

Finally, this game has exceptional graphics and the story has lots of funny moments, as well as scary ones. But, did it make me feel more intelligent? Well, yes, after a few weeks, it did! I started to think about real-life problems in different ways, and realized that there is always more than one way to solve a problem. Not bad for a computer game!

You can download the game now, and we wish you luck in getting to the end! We give *Box of Time* three out of five stars.

🔊 **10.2**

1 Are computer games bad for us?
2 What can we do to make computer games more intelligent?
3 How can computer games keep our brains healthy and active?
4 What does it all mean?
5 Did it make me feel more intelligent?

Name: .... **Date:** ....

LISTENING (20 marks)

LISTENING 1

1 (◀) **1.1**) Listen and underline the stressed syllable in each word. 1 mark for each correct answer.

1 convinced
2 relocated
3 survive
4 communicate
5 poisonous
6 harmless
7 environment
8 treated
9 realize
10 conditions

LISTENING 2

2 (◀) **1.2**) Listen to the recording. Are the statements true (T) or false (F)? 1 mark for each correct answer.

1 The speaker doesn't like dogs. ＿＿
2 He prefers animals to people. ＿＿
3 He has never been to a zoo. ＿＿
4 He had a pet dog when he was younger. ＿＿
5 He wasn't happy when his pet became ill. ＿＿
6 He never played with his pet. ＿＿
7 He wanted to have another pet. ＿＿
8 His son would like a pet. ＿＿
9 He doesn't want an exotic pet. ＿＿
10 He thinks that people should not buy pets from shops. ＿＿

LANGUAGE DEVELOPMENT (15 marks)

3 Complete the table. 1 mark for each correct answer.

noun	verb	adjective
1 _____	analyze	analytical
environment		2 _____
3 _____	communicate	communicating
4 _____	involve	involved
5 _____	abuse	abused

4 Complete the sentences below with a word from the table in Exercise 3. 1 mark for each correct answer.

1 Men need to become more _____ in the raising of their children.

2 After years of _____, it now looks as though these poor animals have finally found a new home.

3 Ms Graham, what's your _____ of the current situation? How are things likely to develop?

4 Unless world leaders are prepared to do something to fight global warming, we really do face an _____ disaster.

5 The smartphone is by far the most popular means of _____ ever.

5 Are the sentences true (T) or false (F)? 1 mark for each correct answer.

1 Things described as *domestic* are to do with the home or with your own country. ___

2 Zoology is the study of plant life. ___

3 If you abandon something, then you leave it for a short time. ___

4 A savannah is a large area of grassy land in a hot area. ___

5 If something is harmless, then it can hurt you. ___

TOTAL ___ / 35

REVIEW TEST 2

Name: .... **Date:** ....

LISTENING (20 marks)

LISTENING 1

1 (◀) 2.1) Listen to the recording. Underline the 't' in each sentence which you can hear pronounced clearly. 1 mark for each correct answer.

1 What was so good about Austria?

2 There are great summers, and spring is just amazing.

3 Was it a festival or was it something else?

4 What happens in this festival – what are the people doing?

5 People wear a lot of different things.

LISTENING 2

2 (◀) 2.2) Listen to the recording. Are the statements true (T) or false (F)? 1 mark for each correct answer.

1 One of the speakers is living in Austria at the moment. ___

2 The main topic of the conversation is about the Austrian countryside. ___

3 Martha is the name given to five villages in Austria. ___

4 The speaker stayed in a village. ___

5 The Mullers are a family in Austria. ___

6 The Mullers wear masks made of wood. ___

7 During the carnival season, Austrians usually dress up as ghosts and monsters. ___

8 In the larger villages, people only wear traditional costumes. ___

9 Only old people take part in the carnival. ___

10 The speaker took part in the celebration. ___

3 (◀) 2.2) Listen again and complete the sentences with the words in the box. You do not need every word. 1 mark for each correct answer.

alive behaviour special traditional generations anniversary identity out complicated

1 Each village has a strong _____.

2 All the different _____ take part in the carnival.

3 The speaker thinks it's good that this local tradition is being kept _____.

4 In the smaller villages, you can see more _____ clothes.

5 The *Muller* represent the four seasons, and each has a different pattern of _____ .

LANGUAGE DEVELOPMENT (15 marks)

4 The words in bold below have the wrong suffix. Correct the mistakes using the word forms in brackets. 1 mark for each correct answer.

1 The book didn't help at all. It's totally **using**. _____ (adverb)

2 Our region has some very interesting **tradition** music. _____ (adjective)

3 We should be **care** to preserve our way of life. _____ (adjective)

4 I've had a very **enjoy** time, thanks! _____ (adjective)

5 We're going to have a big **celebrate** next month. _____ (noun)

5 Correct the spelling mistakes. 1 mark for each correct answer.

1 sociel ___

2 threwout ___

3 aniversary ___

4 afect ___

5 globel ___

6 Are the sentences true (T) or false (F)? 1 mark for each correct answer.

1 Anthropology is the study of humans. ___

2 If you adapt, then you never change. ___

3 An event is a thing that happens or takes place. ___

4 If you spread something, you extend it over a large area. ___

5 If something keeps off, then it is no longer alive. ___

TOTAL ___ / 35

REVIEW TEST 3

Name: .... Date: ....

LISTENING (20 marks)

LISTENING 1

1 (◀) 3.1) Listen to the recording. Underline the words pronounced as weak forms (/ə/) in each sentence. 1 mark for each correct sentence.

 1 We've got to give a presentation about a person from history.
 2 Plato said that she was one of the greatest poets he had read.
 3 She was a British women's rights activist who lived in the late 1900s.
 4 Have you heard of her?
 5 That was the start of the equal rights movement in America.

LISTENING 2

2 (◀) 3.2) Listen to the recording. Are the sentences true (T) or false (F)? 1 mark for each correct answer.

 1 The discussion is between two colleagues. ___
 2 They have been asked to give a presentation about a historical person. ___
 3 They think that most famous people in the past were women. ___
 4 Sappho wrote her poems 200 years ago. ___
 5 Emmeline Pankhurst was one of the first female politicians. ___
 6 She never voted. ___
 7 Rosa Parks never wanted to become famous. ___
 8 She didn't stand up on the bus. ___
 9 In the 1950s, it was shocking for a Black person to give their seat to a White person. ___
 10 Gemma and Susan decide not to talk about one historical person. ___

3 (◀) 3.2) Listen again and complete each sentence with one word. You do not need to use all the words. 1 mark for each correct answer.

 1 Most _____ in the past were men.
 2 Sappho lived in _____ Greece.
 3 Emmeline Pankhurst had a _____ effect on British women.
 4 In the _____ of 1950s America, Black people did not have equal rights with White people.
 5 Gemma and Susan promise to _____ information after doing more research.

LANGUAGE DEVELOPMENT (15 marks)

4 Complete the sentences with *which*, *where* or *who*. 1 mark for each correct answer.

1 Bavaria, _____ is now part of Germany, used to be an independent kingdom.

2 The place _____ you can see the famous Leonardo fresco is in Milan.

3 Victoria, _____ was queen of Great Britain and Ireland and empress of India, died in 1901.

4 The Deutsches Museum, _____ you can see many exhibits from the world of science and technology, is in Munich.

5 The British museum, _____ contains many treasures, is in London.

5 For each sentence, choose one word or phrase from the box that can replace one word in the sentence. You do not need to use all the words. 1 mark for each correct answer.

> lots   army   discovered   youthful   soldiers
> ancient   ruler

1 She found the treasure while digging in her garden. _____

2 He sent his warriors across Europe, conquering every country in their path. _____

3 At the time of his death, he was the oldest Emperor the world had ever known. _____

4 There are plenty of books there to keep you busy. You should be able to find everything you need. _____

5 So just how many of these old statues are there on the island? _____

6 Choose the correct word/phrase in each sentence. 1 mark for each correct sentence.

1 The 1960s was a very good *decade / century* for music.

2 He was born in the *early / late* 1800s – in 1896, to be exact.

3 The Middle Ages is also known as the *mid / medieval* period.

4 He started playing the piano *at the age / at that time* of five.

5 She was very worried about her exams, because *a short while later / at that time* she hadn't studied very much.

TOTAL ___ / 35

Name: .... Date: ....

LISTENING (20 marks)

LISTENING 1

1 (🔊 4.1) Listen and choose the correct answer (a, b or c). 1 mark for each correct answer.

1 Who are the speakers?
   a friends
   b relatives
   c colleagues

2 What are they worried about?
   a accidents at work
   b the dangers of texting while walking
   c problems at school

3 Why do road accidents involving children double at the age of 11?
   a because many children walk to school at that age
   b because that is when children get their first mobile phone
   c because 11 year olds can't concentrate very well

4 Why did one of the speakers buy mobile phones for his children?
   a because the school asked him to do it
   b as a present
   c because all of the children's friends had mobile phones

5 Who do they think should teach children to use mobile phones safely?
   a schools
   b parents
   c both parents and schools

2 (🔊 4.1) Listen again. Are the statements true (T) or false (F)? 1 mark for each correct answer.

1 The speakers don't think that texting while walking is a serious problem. ___
2 The speakers both agree that mobile phones should include safety features for parents to use. ___
3 They think that children will easily learn to switch off a safety feature. ___
4 One of the speaker's children caused a car crash. ___
5 One of the speakers has children who are around 11 years old. ___
6 Children around the age of 11–12 are twice as likely to be involved in car accidents. ___
7 One speaker says that most children don't really want a mobile phone. ___
8 One speakers says that car drivers should be more careful. ___
9 The speakers think that it's not possible to make texting while walking a criminal offence. ___
10 They both agree on who should take responsibility for the problem. ___

LISTENING 2

3 (◄) **4.2** Listen to the recording. For each of the bolded words, underline the stressed syllable. 1 mark for each correct answer.

1 Some people did **research** into accidents involving children who text while walking.
2 I bought my kids mobiles as a **present** for their birthdays, so I could keep in touch with them.
3 Why the **increase** in accidents?
4 We need to **decrease the number of accidents**.
5 Schools can't **control** what the kids are doing in their own free time – that's down to the parents.

LANGUAGE DEVELOPMENT (15 marks)

4 Complete the sentences below with the correct form of the adjectives in brackets. 1 mark for each correct answer.

1 In a big city, driving a car is often _____ than riding a bicycle. (slow)
2 It is _____ not to text while walking. (good)
3 That article is rather boring. This one is much _____ . (interesting)
4 I find that taking the train is _____ way to travel. (comfortable)
5 It is _____ to take the bus than spend ages trying to find a parking space. (easy)

5 Complete the sentences with the correct form of the words from the box. You do not need to use all the words. 1 mark for each correct answer.

| injure experience relax crash challenge |
| goal damage safety attitude |

1 A good massage will _____ your tired muscles.
2 He was badly _____ in the crash.
3 Finding a solution to this problem is one of the greatest _____ faced by scientists today.
4 Both the cars involved in the accident looked badly _____ .
5 They have set themselves a series of _____ to achieve by the end of the month.

6 Each sentence contains a spelling mistake. Correct the wrong word. 1 mark for each correct answer.

1 It's often very difficult to change people's atitudes. _____
2 I like the convience of living so near to work. _____
3 She finally acheived her ambition to visit South America. _____
4 Wood, coal, oil, petrol and gas are all different kinds of fule. _____
5 We might be experiencing some turbalance on this flight due to an approaching electrical storm. _____

TOTAL ___ / 35

Name: .... **Date:** ....

LISTENING (20 marks)

LISTENING 1

1 (◀) 5.1) Listen to the recording. Are the statements true (T) or false (F)? 1 mark for each correct answer.

1 The radio program is on the topic of the environment. ___
2 Mrs Trellis thinks climate change has a negative impact. ___
3 The presenter thinks that climate change means that the temperature will only get warmer. ___
4 Robert Shaw thinks that scientists don't focus enough on Europe or North America. ___
5 The presenter thinks that there are not so many hurricanes now, because of climate change. ___
6 Ms Tyler doesn't think that climate change will create medical problems. ___
7 Ms Tyler believes that climate change will have an impact on food supplies. ___
8 Saffron thinks that the planet is in safe hands. ___

2 (◀) 5.1) Listen again. Complete the notes with one word in each gap. 1 mark for each correct answer.

One reason that temperatures are going up is because of (1)_____ gases.
The presenter thinks that Mrs Trellis has an (2)_____ attitude.
Even a small rise in temperature could have very bad (3)_____ effects.
Robert Shaw thinks that there is (4)_____ between scientists on the subject of climate change.
He says that scientists are focusing too much on countries which have an (5)_____ climate.
Ms Tyler is worried that there might be an increase in (6)_____ like malaria.
Saffron doesn't believe a warmer (7)_____ is better and says it would be good if fossil (8)_____ could be banned.

LISTENING 2

3 (◀) 5.2) Listen to the recording. What sound can you hear between the words in bold in each sentence? Write /r/ or /w/. 1 mark for each correct answer.

1 I heard that temperatures might **go up** because of greenhouse gases. _____
2 But **there is** a lot of disagreement as to whether or not it's a bad thing. _____
3 The debate **too often** centres around areas of extreme climate, like in Africa. _____
4 Malaria, **for example**, is one disease which might become more common. _____

LANGUAGE DEVELOPMENT (15 marks)

4 Use the negative prefixes in the box to make new words. You will not need to use all of the prefixes. 1 mark for each correct answer.

anti il ir de im mis un in

1 ____responsible

2 ____clockwise

3 ____experienced

4 ____mature

5 ____treat

5 Choose the correct modal verb to express the meaning in the brackets. 1 mark for each correct answer.

1 Alternative energy sources *will / might* be cheaper in the future. (a possible future)

2 Burning fossil fuels *will / could* increase global warming. (certainty in the future)

3 Reducing car use *may not / can't* be done easily. (certainty in the future)

4 Further research into renewable energy *will / may* help us in the future. (softer opinion)

5 In the next few years, solar energy *will / could* be the best solution to global warming. (a possible future)

6 Unscramble the words in bold. 1 mark for each correct answer.

1 There has never been a nuclear **redssait** in this country. _____

2 If we rely only on alternative energy, our economy will be at a serious **sdatagdnavie**. _____

3 The only **rcbadwka** with solar energy is that it is expensive. _____

4 There are many **ebtnfies** to reducing the amount of energy you use. _____

5 In the future, oil will become less **fafrobadel**. _____

TOTAL ___ / 35

REVIEW TEST 6

Name: .... **Date:** ....

LISTENING (20 marks)

LISTENING 1

1 (◀) 6.1) Listen to the recording and choose the correct answer (a, b or c). 1 mark for each correct answer.

1 Who are the speakers?

    a a brother and a sister

    b a worker and his boss

    c two friends

2 When did the two last see each other?

    a a long time ago

    b yesterday

    c last week

3 Why doesn't Lauren take regular exercise?

    a She is slim and doesn't need to work out.

    b She has no time.

    c She has bad knees.

4 Why did Mark stop exercising 15 years ago?

    a He got an office job.

    b He met his wife.

    c He had a baby.

5 Why does he want to get fit now?

    a for his job

    b so he can exercise with his son

    c for his father

6 How much exercise does Mark get a day?

    a 15–30 minutes

    b 45 minutes

    c 60 minutes

7 Who looks after Ben in the morning?

    a Mark's wife

    b Mark

    c They have a nanny.

8 Why is the cross trainer good for Mark?

    a He can exercise at home when he wants.

    b He can watch TV all day.

    c He doesn't want to go to the gym.

9 How much does Mark weigh now?
  a 95 kilos
  b 75 kilos
  c 45 kilos
10 Why will Mark keep his cross trainer once he's reached his goal?
  a No one else wants it.
  b It is too big to move easily.
  c He's worried he might get fat again.

2 (◀)) 6.1) Listen again. Are the statements true (T) or false (F)? 1 mark for each correct answer.
  1 Mark hasn't been to the gym recently. ___
  2 Mark hasn't lost any weight recently. ___
  3 Mark thinks that he is overweight. ___
  4 Lauren doesn't like exercising. ___
  5 Mark has been a dad for a long time. ___
  6 Mark likes playing with his son. ___
  7 Mark doesn't exercise while his son is asleep. ___
  8 Mark exercises at different times during the day. ___
  9 Mark has an exercise plan. ___
  10 Lauren is interested in Mark's cross trainer. ___

LANGUAGE DEVELOPMENT (15 marks)

3 Complete the phrasal verbs with one word. 1 mark for each correct answer.
  1 Hey, you're looking great! Have you been working _____?
  2 She's signed _____ for a yoga class, starting next week.
  3 I couldn't exercise because I had a bad cold – it went _____ for two weeks.
  4 If you want to do a marathon, then you have to give _____ bad foods – sugar, fat, and so on.
  5 Exercise has taken _____ his life – he's running and cycling every day!
  6 I was brought _____ in a sporty family, so it's not surprising that I became a sports teacher.
  7 I couldn't make _____ what the fitness instructor was saying, because the music in the gym was too loud.
  8 I'm thinking of taking _____ a new sport – what do you recommend?
  9 My car has broken _____ – that's why I'm using my bike.
  10 It takes a long time to get _____ a muscle injury.

4 Unscramble the words in bold. 1 mark for each correct sentence. _____
  1 I know I should exercise **rglaerluy**, but I don't have time. _____
  2 Eating chocolate is a bad **abhti** which I'd like to stop. _____
  3 I always check the **ninedtriegs** before I buy food. _____
  4 It's not **uatarln** to stay indoors all day, playing computer games. _____
  5 He says he's **worvegeith** but I think he looks fine. _____

TOTAL ___ / 35

REVIEW TEST 7

Name: .... Date: ....

LISTENING (20 marks)

LISTENING 1

1 (◀) **7.1** Listen to the recording. Are the sentences true (T) or false (F)? 1 mark for each correct answer.

1 The programme is about old mechanical toys. ___

2 The presenters are talking about their own childhood toy. ___

3 Jeannie's toy used to be popular in the past. ___

4 This toy helped children to learn. ___

5 Jeannie bought her toy in a second-hand shop. ___

6 You spoke to the toy, and it repeated what you said. ___

7 The toy once appeared in a film. ___

8 Jeannie had no problem understanding the toy. ___

9 Her spelling is very good now. ___

10 Children nowadays would probably use a spelling game on a mobile phone. ___

2 (◀) **7.1** Listen again and choose the correct answer (a, b or c). 1 mark for each correct answer.

1 Why does the male presenter speak like a robot?

  a because the guest has a toy that sounds similar

  b to make his co-presenter laugh

  c because he has forgotten what he is supposed to say

2 When was Jeannie's toy first produced?

  a in the 1970s

  b in the 1980s

  c in the 1990s

3 How did the machine work?

  a You said a word, and it showed you the spelling.

  b It said a word, and you typed it in.

  c It said a word, and you repeated it.

4 Why did Jeannie sometimes find it difficult to understand the toy?

  a because she words were too difficult

  b because she was bad at spelling

  c because the machine spoke with a different accent

5 What does she think about computer games and mobile phones?

  a Children don't use them for learning.

  b You should only use them when you are young.

  c They are useful for helping children to learn to spell.

LISTENING 2

3 (🔊 7.2) Listen to the recording. Are the words in bold pronounced as strong form? Write yes (Y) or no (N). 1 mark for each correct answer.

  1 Yes, there certainly **are**. _____
  2 The Speak & Spell toys **were** very popular throughout the 1980s. _____
  3 It **was** designed to teach children to spell. _____
  4 What **do** you think about that? _____
  5 I **do** believe that anything that helps you practise your spelling when you are young is great. _____

LANGUAGE DEVELOPMENT (15 marks)

4 Complete the sentences with the words from the box. You will not need all the words. 1 mark for each correct answer.

> believe discovery sure mistake friends
> difference time mind

  1 Please try not to make the same _____ during your final exam!
  2 Can one person really make such a _____ to the world?
  3 It was in this room that Marie Curie made her amazing _____.
  4 Can you make up your _____ soon? I don't have much time!
  5 I need to make _____ the results are correct before sending them in.

5 Complete the sentences using the correct form of the verbs in the brackets. Use active or passive forms. 1 mark for each correct answer.

  1 The diamonds _____ (discover) in 1972.
  2 The game _____ (invented) by schoolchildren in Australia.
  3 We _____ (develop) the smartphone app as part of a national competition.
  4 The first email _____ (sent) in 1971.
  5 William Moggridge _____ (design) one of the first laptops in 1979.

6 Are the sentences true (T) or false (F)? 1 mark for each correct answer.

  1 If you recommend something, then you say it is good. ___
  2 If a product is available, then you can't buy it yet. ___
  3 If your train is delayed then you will arrive sooner. ___
  4 A phenomenon is an unusual or surprising event. ___
  5 When a product is launched, it is no longer possible to buy it. ___

TOTAL ___ / 35

Name: ....   Date: ....

LISTENING (20 marks)

LISTENING 1

1 (◀) **8.1** Listen to the recording. Are the statements true (T) or false (F)? 1 mark for each correct answer.

   1 The UK is becoming increasingly fashion-conscious. ____

   2 The idea for the research came from a magazine. ____

   3 According to the survey, the UK was more fashion-conscious than the US. ____

   4 People who live in the UK are becoming much larger than they were before. ____

   5 It is becoming more difficult for overweight people to find good clothes. ____

   6 Fashion companies are becoming more interested in making clothes for larger people. ____

   7 Britain will become more fashion-conscious in the future. ____

2 (◀) **8.1** Listen again and choose the correct answer (a, b or c). 1 mark for each correct answer.

   1 Which of these was <u>not</u> used to find out how fashion-conscious the UK was?

     a internet posts   b sales of clothing   c asking people questions

   2 What did the readers of *Looks!* magazine say?

     a that they cared less about fashion than before

     b that people still cared about fashion

     c that, in general, people cared less about fashion than before

   3 How fashion-conscious is the UK compared to the rest of Europe?

     a less   b more   c no information available

   4 What does 17.8% refer to?

     a how many people answered the survey

     b the decrease in 'being fashionable' from two years ago

     c the percentage of people who buy fashionable clothes

   5 How does Judy Hubbard explain the data she has for the UK?

     a people are wearing more sports clothing

     b people have less money available

     c people are getting fatter

   6 What are the 'lifestyle choices' that Judy talks about?

     a buying clothes   b eating more   c doing sports

   7 Why did many British people buy sportswear in the past?

     a because it looked good on larger people

     b because they were very sporty

     c because they were the most fashionable clothes

   8 What are fashion companies concentrating on now, according to Judy?

     a larger people   b pop stars   c sports people

LISTENING 2

3 (◀ 8.2) Listen to the recording. Complete each sentence with one word. 1 mark for each correct answer.

1 This year, you're 17.8% less likely to see _____ clothing than last year.

2 It is the result of information collected from photos we took with our own _____.

3 So, why are things _____?

4 I don't think people are going to get thinner, _____.

5 Well, that's certainly an _____ point of view.

LANGUAGE DEVELOPMENT (15 marks)

4 Choose the word that best completes each sentence. 1 mark for each correct answer.

1 I'm quite interested in computers, technology, and all *this / that*.

2 As far as I'm *concerned / certain*, digital media is not just the future. It's the present.

3 I read it last year. I wasn't *angry / mad* about it, but my husband thought it was great.

4 I'm not sure I can finish this on my own. Can you give me a *hand / finger*?

5 It's not really my kind of thing, but I still went – just for *fun / funny*.

5 Complete the sentences with the most likely future form. 1 mark for each correct answer.

1 We'd better take an umbrella. I think *it's going to rain / it rains*.

2 My train *is arriving / arrives* at exactly 9.45.

3 We *have / are having* a party at the end of the semester. It'd be great if you could come.

4 I'm not feeling well – I think *I'll / I'm going to* call in sick.

5 A: I'm taking the bus, so may be a few minutes late.

   B: The buses don't run on Sunday.

   A: OK, *I'll drive / I'm driving* then. See you later!

6 Read the discussion between two colleagues. Circle the phrase that best completes each sentence. 1 mark for each correct answer.

A: (1) *Would you say that / What do you think* is the best way to get to the city centre?

B: I usually take the bus. Then you don't have to worry about parking.

A: (2) *Would you say that / How do you feel about* the new pedestrian area?

B: I think it's great. There's less noise, more shops and I love the new terrace cafés that have opened since cars were banned. (3) *Don't you agree? / What do you mean?*

A: I'm not sure. I think it's bad for business. It makes things more difficult for people to deliver goods. It's also now difficult for people who want to do a big shop.

B: (4) *Do you mean that / What's your opinion about* cars should be allowed back into town?

A: No. But they should certainly be able to park closer than they can now.

B: (5) *I see what you mean / I disagree*. But I quite like the walk from the bus stop. Especially if you go along the river.

TOTAL ___ / 35

REVIEW TEST 9

Name: .... **Date:** ....

LISTENING (20 marks)

LISTENING 1

1 (9.1) Listen to the recording and choose the correct answer (a, b or c). 1 mark for each correct answer.

1 What research is being carried out?
   a research into who uses public transport
   b research into whether people like public transport
   c research into how much people spend on public transport

2 What type of transport does the interviewee use?
   a car and bus
   b train
   c car and train

3 How often does the interviewee use public transport?
   a once or twice a week
   b every day except weekends
   c every day

4 How much money does the interviewee spend on commuting?
   a more than he would like
   b a small amount
   c nothing

5 Why is the interviewee generally negative about public transport?
   a It's too dirty.
   b It isn't good value for money.
   c The car is cheaper.

2 (9.1) Listen again. Are the statements true (T) or false (F)? 1 mark for each correct answer.

1 The interviewee has lots of time. ____
2 The train prices have increased recently. ____
3 The quality of the trains has not increased. ____
4 The interviewee thinks it's necessary to use public transport. ____
5 The trains are usually comfortable, and the interviewee can get a seat. ____
6 Driving to work would be slower than taking the train. ____
7 The interviewee sometimes travels first class. ____
8 Travelling by train costs a lot of money. ____
9 Public transport will get cheaper in the future. ____
10 The interviewee doesn't have time to talk any more because his train is about to arrive. ____

LISTENING 2

3 ◀) **9.2** Listen and complete the sentences with words that you hear. 1 mark for each correct answer.

1 I hope I can _____ them, but I need to go in five minutes.
2 And it was _____, because I don't think the quality of the service went up.
3 A: And how much of your income is taken up by commuting?
   B: I don't know _____.
4 I earn a reasonably income, and have relatively few _____.
5 It's always been like that, and I _____ that it will change in the near future.

LANGUAGE DEVELOPMENT (15 marks)

4 Complete the dialogue with the words and phrases from the box. You will not need all the words. 1 mark for each correct answer.

> cash fines borrow bills debt lend
> credit card

1 Bob: Can I pay by _____?
2 Waiter: Sorry, in _____only.
3 Bob: Oh dear. Hang on a minute. Er, Rita – can you _____ me any money?
4 Rita: It's OK. I'll pay the _____.

5 Choose the correct words. 1 mark for each correct answer.

1 You can *save / pay* a lot of time if you don't check your email so often.
2 Meral *lost / paid* a lot of money to her dentist, but it was worth it.
3 I want to *earn / save* money for a new car.
4 He never *pays / saves* attention in class.
5 My sister *borrowed / lent* me some money to start up my own business.
6 After my presentation, my friend *paid / lent* me a compliment and said it was very interesting.

6 Match the sentence beginnings to the sentence endings.

1 If you want to buy a new house,
2 If you want to be rich,
3 If you want to get a better job,
4 If you wear expensive clothes,
5 If I have money at the end of the week,

a you need to work hard, every day.
b people will think you are rich.
c I will buy myself a new shirt.
d you have to save a lot of money.
e you should send your CV to lots of companies.

TOTAL ___ / 35

REVIEW TEST 10

Name: .... **Date:** ....

LISTENING (20 marks)

LISTENING 1

1 (◀) **10.1** Listen to the recording. Are the sentences true (T) or false (F)? 1 mark for each correct answer.

1 The podcast is about new computer games and software. ___

2 The reviewer thinks that some computer games can help you learn. ___

3 *Annie Pond and the Box of Time* is the same as any other action game. ___

4 You can finish this game very quickly. ___

5 Annie Pond is a character in the game. ___

6 The game gets easier, the more time you spend on it. ___

7 *Box of Time* is good for people who like brain exercises. ___

8 The program's images are not very good. ___

9 The game is good for people with different styles of thinking. ___

10 The reviewer thinks the game helped her become more intelligent. ___

2 (◀) **10.1** Listen again and complete each sentence with one word or phrase you hear. 1 mark for each correct answer.

1 The reviewer thinks that if you don't like computer games, *Annie Pond and the Box of Time* will _____.

2 It is a _____ game, different from all the other games.

3 The main character in the game is a _____ teenage detective who solves crimes.

4 You need to _____ to the game as you play, and it will change the way you think.

5 The graphics in the game are _____.

LISTENING 2

3 (◀) **10.2** Listen to the recording. Does the intonation go up ↑ or down ↓ at the end of each question? 1 mark for each correct answer.

1 Are computer games bad for us? _____

2 What can we do to make computer games more intelligent? _____

3 How can computer games keep our brains healthy and active? _____

4 What does it all mean? _____

5 Did it make me feel more intelligent? _____

LANGUAGE DEVELOPMENT (15 marks)

4 Complete the collocations with *mind* collocations. 1 mark for each correct answer.

1 A: Are you still going to Stockholm for the summer?

   B: No. I've _____ my mind. I've just booked a week in Paris.

2 A: Hi! Oh, what a beautiful bunch of flowers! Who are they from?

   B: Mind your own _____!

   A: Hey! No need to be like that!

   B: I was joking! But I still won't tell you who sent them!

3 A: Sorry I'm late, we were snowed in.

   B: _____ mind. We started the meeting without you.

4 A: Charles, do you _____ something on your mind? You've been acting strangely all evening.

   B: Oh Fiona! It's James. He called to say the deal's off. I'm so terribly sorry.

5 A: Shall we take this flight or the earlier one?

   B: I don't care. But you should _____ up your mind soon or there'll be no seats left.

6 A: Don't forget – you have an exam next month, so you should study.

   B: OK, yes. I'll _____ it in mind.

7 A: Excuse me, _____ you mind opening the window?

   B: No, of course not.

8 A: I find it difficult to say what I really want to say.

   B: I know. You really need to learn to _____ you mind.

5 Each sentence contains one spelling mistake. Correct the spelling mistakes. 1 mark for each correct answer.

1 The accident occured at 11:30 pm. _____

2 Some animals, like dogs or dolphins, are actually quite inteligent. _____

3 There is a new teory that computer games can help you learn. _____

4 Even ordnary minds are capable of doing amazing things. _____

5 We need to find a way to work more effisently. _____

6 I conducted a survey to detemine whether children really do learn languages more quickly than adults. _____

7 There have been many exprements on the human brain. _____

TOTAL ___ / 35

ADDITIONAL SPEAKING TASK 1

> **Do you like working with animals?** Full-time work available over the busy summer season. The position involves feeding the animals, cleaning the animal enclosures and answering visitors' questions. Experience with animals would be an advantage.

Interviewers

Student A: Zoo general manager

You will interview the candidates together with the head zookeeper. You want to find out:

- why they want the job
- what experience they have in working with tourists
- what they think about zoos
- if they'd like a full-time position.

Student B: Head zookeeper

You will interview the candidates together with the general manager. You want to find out:

- what experience they have with animals
- what qualities they feel are important for the job
- if they would be interested in full-time work
- how well they speak English.

Interviewees

Student C

You have applied for a position at the local zoo in the summer holidays. You have little experience with animals, but did once feed your aunt's dog while she was away. You think that zoos are important for research and nature conservation, and would be interested in working full-time after your studies if you are unable to find an office job. Your English is quite good, and last year you worked as a tour guide in your hometown.

Student D

You have applied for a position at the local zoo in the summer holidays. Last year, you worked part-time at a safari park, although you left the job to continue your studies. When you were younger, you believed that all zoos should be closed down because they were an unnatural environment for animals. However, you now think that zoos are beneficial. You would like to work with animals following your studies. Your English is quite good, and you have many English friends.

MODEL LANGUAGE

Expressing obligation and giving suggestions

You have to love animals to do this job.

You must have experience of dealing with tourists.

You should have a positive attitude towards zoos.

You need to be polite to the visitors.

You ought to have experience with animals.

Introducing examples

I have experience working with animals. For example, I used to work at a safari park.

I think zoos are important. For instance, they are useful for research and nature conservation.

I think zoos can help endangered animals, such as the giant panda or the leopard.

Contrasting ideas

Even though I don't have a lot of experience, I would love to do this job.

I don't have much experience with animals. Yet, I do have experience of working with tourists.

When I was younger, I didn't like zoos. However, I now think that they are very important.

ADDITIONAL SPEAKING TASK 2

Think of a tradition that is dying out in your country, or everywhere, and discuss these points.

• What are the reasons that this tradition is dying out?

• Should anything be done to preserve it?

• If yes, what? If no, why not?

MODEL LANGUAGE

Identifying cause and effect

Some traditions die out because of new ways of life.

More people are using the internet. That's why families can live further apart.

Now, due to developments in technology, people spend more time playing games on their phones.

But now we don't have to work so hard. The reason for this is that we have modern kitchens and supermarket food.

You can find any recipe you want on the internet. This means that many people don't need cookbooks anymore.

Taking turns in a discussion

What do you think?

I see your point, but …

I totally agree.

I'm really not convinced.

I'm sorry to interrupt, but …

You may be right but …

Phrases with *that* to introduce an opinion or idea

I've heard that …

Everyone knows that …

It's a well-known fact that …

I doubt that …

I strongly believe that …

ADDITIONAL SPEAKING TASK 3

The new education secretary has said that schools are not doing enough to prepare students for the workplace. She has suggested stopping the teaching of History after the age of 12 and replacing it with more useful subjects, such as IT or Business Studies.

Student A

You believe that there is no point in teaching History. It should be left for universities to offer to students who wish to follow an academic career. You think that pupils should be encouraged to learn more vocational skills that reflect the needs of industry. If children really want to learn about the past, they can find all the information they could ever need online.

Student B

You are a History teacher and are passionate about your subject. You believe that History is about far more than studying the past. It helps children understand why their country is the way it is, as well as teaching them about other cultures. Studying History also teaches children the difference between facts and opinions, and cause and effect. These skills are important in the workplace.

Student C

You are pleased that, under the new scheme, pupils will still be required to study History until the age of 12. However, you think that children should be free to decide whether or not they should study History beyond that age. Teaching this subject should not be stopped, but it should not be compulsory after the age of 12.

MODEL LANGUAGE

Showing that you are paying attention

I see.

What do you think?

Yes, you're right.

Yes. I know what you mean.

That's a good idea.

Yes, exactly.

Using relative clauses

This is not a subject which many children are interested in.

History can teach you many skills which are useful for your later career.

Sequencing words and phrases

Children can learn about their country. Meanwhile, they can also learn about the difference between facts and opinions, and the importance of cause and effect.

If children study History, then eventually, they will develop a lot of useful skills.

During my time at school, I never studied much History.

ADDITIONAL SPEAKING TASK 4

You have been asked to give your opinion about a new law which will encourage car sharing. This will involve more than one family regularly using the same car, encouraging people to take more passengers, or both. The more people in one car, the less road tax the driver will have to pay.

Student A

You are a self-employed plumber. You rely on your van for work, and have a car for personal use. You think that road tax should be cheaper for people who regularly drive to work with passengers, but people should not be penalized if they drive a vehicle not suitable for taking passengers.

Student B

You sell cars. You think that car sharing is not a good idea. People should be free to drive alone if they want. You are prepared to accept higher road taxes for a second car bought only for personal use.

Student C

You are an environmental activist. You believe that road taxes on all cars should be doubled, and that cars should never be used if they carry fewer than three people (unless in emergencies). You would use the money raised through increased taxes to develop a better public transport system.

Student D

You are a student. You regularly share your car with other students, and could not afford to run it without the shared petrol money. You know that it is possible to share cars, and think that other drivers should be encouraged to do this.

MODEL LANGUAGE

Comparing things

The road tax will be a <u>lot</u> more than I expected.

This is by far the best idea.

This would be considerably more difficult.

Cars are much more comfortable than public transport.

Sharing a car is definitely more practical in a big city than in the country.

Proposing ideas

I think it would be safer if …

In my opinion, we should …

I'd like it if …

(They) ought to …

The best thing would be if …

I think it would be much better if …

(They) should …

I'd like to see more …

I'd suggest …

Expanding on an idea

I don't think the government should do anything about it.

Personally, I …

This is because …

From my own experience, …

The best thing would be to …

The reason for this is …

ADDITIONAL SPEAKING TASK 5

The *Love Food, Hate Waste* campaign was launched in 2007 to highlight the problem of food waste in the UK, first identified as a serious problem in 1915. A major source of food waste in the UK is the 6,700,000 tonnes of potatoes, bread, apples and other foodstuffs thrown away by households. Discuss the advantages and disadvantages of these suggestions as to how to reduce household waste, and decide which ones should be pursued.

- Banning *best before* dates.
- Stopping supermarkets selling 'two-for-one' offers.
- Creating new food-packaging sizes.
- Encouraging people to donate unwanted food to food banks.
- Encouraging people to learn to cook more effectively.

MODEL LANGUAGE

Modals to express opinions

Banning *best before* dates is a good idea.

This might be a good solution.

This could be effective.

Supermarkets will not be happy with this solution.

Linking ideas

To begin with, I think supermarkets should …

On the other hand, we should think about …

I don't think we waste as much food in comparison with the UK.

As well as that, we should think about …

Overall, we need to find a solution to …

Talking about advantages

In my opinion, there are many pros.

Personally, I think that this would have a negative effect.

The good thing about this is that …

The main benefit of this is that …

There are many cons of doing this.

The main drawback of this is that …

ADDITIONAL SPEAKING TASK 6

> Many people would like to be healthier and fitter, but never have time to do enough sport or eat properly. Diets come and go; new fitness fashions become very popular and then disappear overnight.

Prepare a new fitness programme:

- include tips on good nutrition
- make it easy to follow
- focus on sports and exercises that everyone can do with minimal equipment and without needing to join a gym
- consider how affordable your ideas are and how easily available the food that you recommend is
- consider the other factors that prevent people from keeping fit
- develop your programme with the needs of an office worker with little free time in mind.

MODEL LANGUAGE

Referring to common knowledge

Everyone knows that …
We all know that …
Most people think that …
There is no doubt that …
There is no question that …

Talking about preferences

I'd prefer to exercise and eat well than be unhealthy.
Most people would rather go out and have a pizza with friends than spend time in the gym.

Using imperatives to persuade

Try our new fitness programme.
Buy one, get one free.
Hurry and book (a ticket) now.
Don't forget that our …
Join our courses before it's too late!

ADDITIONAL SPEAKING TASK 7

You are researchers working for a new TV series about technology. You have been asked to prepare a programme called *Inventions: The top 10.* Your job is to make a list of inventions which could be included on this list. These should be the most important inventions created in the last 100 years. These are inventions that it would be impossible to imagine life without. You should put the inventions in the order of importance (1 = most important) and be prepared to give reasons for your choices.

Prepare a two-minute presentation of your ideas.

MODEL LANGUAGE

Passive verb forms

… was discovered in …

… was invented in …

… was brought to … from …

… was first made in …

Outlining a topic

I would like to present …

I'm going to briefly talk about …

I'd like to start by … / First, I am going to talk about …

We will then … / Then, I will explain how …

Organizing ideas

Now, I'd like to mention …

In the next part of this presentation, I will discuss …

Explaining how something is used

It allows us to …

It helps people to …

It's useful for …

It makes it easy to …

Without …, we wouldn't be able to …

ADDITIONAL SPEAKING TASK 8

Student A: Robin Soft

You are a TV journalist with a gentle approach to interviews. You know little about fashion, and prefer to focus on your interviewees' personal lives. Whenever your interviewees try to talk about fashion, do what you can to get them to talk about something else. Include questions about:

- their favourite colours
- how they get their ideas
- what they do to relax.

Student C: A talented, but unknown, fashion designer

You are a talented designer but not very well-known. You see this interview as an excellent opportunity to talk about your work. If all goes well during the interview, you could become more famous. Take every opportunity to tell viewers how good your designs are, and how much happier their lives would be if they wore your clothes.

Student B: Jamie Strong

You are a journalist with a tough approach to interviews. You research your subjects thoroughly and have strong views on fashion. You think student C could be successful but is too lazy. You think student D is not as talented as people think and doesn't deserve success. Try to keep the interview focused on fashion and away from the interviewees' personal lives. Include questions about:

- their work
- the clothes they are wearing today
- how fashion has changed over the years
- the future of fashion.

Student D: A famous fashion designer

You are a well-known fashion designer, but have not had a new idea in years. Your clothes are still popular because you sell them cheaply to retailers, but you know your best days are behind you. Try to keep the programme focused on you as a well-known 'name' rather than your work as a fashion designer. If the interviewers ask too many questions about fashion, the viewers may think Student C is more talented than you.

MODEL LANGUAGE

Asking for opinions

Can you tell me where you get your ideas from?

How did you feel about … ?

Do you think that … ?

Many reviewers describe your style as 'traditional chic'. Would you agree with this?

What do you think is the best way to … ?

Would you say that … ?

You should look your best. Don't you agree?

Checking information

And what do you think Muslim fashion is?

So are you saying that … ?

As I understand it, your designs are popular outside the US, is that right?

Do you mean that … ?

Focusing on the information coming next

The thing is that …

Let me give you an example …

As far as I'm concerned, …

My feeling is this …

What I think is that …

Another thing is that …

ADDITIONAL SPEAKING TASK 9

You are taking part in a debate on how to raise new taxes. The debate focuses on these questions.

How can the government …

- find new sources of income?
- find ways of saving money?
- be careful not to upset the general population?
- avoid cutting back on essential public services, like schools or hospitals?
- still be popular?

MODEL LANGUAGE

Conditional sentences

If people have a lot of money, they are happier.

If you raise taxes on food, then everyone will notice.

Signalling an opposing point of view

I understand that raising taxes on food will be unpopular. <u>However</u>, …

I can see your point, <u>but</u> …

Asking someone to explain more

Why do you disagree with … ?

Can you explain why … ?

But what if … ?

Why do you think that … ?

What makes you say that … ?

But why shouldn't we … ?

ADDITIONAL SPEAKING TASK 10

Work in groups of 3: A, B and C. Student A should give their opinion about one of the three topics below, and talk uninterrupted for up to two minutes. Student B should then paraphrase what A has said, and then add their own views on the topic. C should then paraphrase what B has said, and then should also give their own opinion. If you have time, you could also choose a second topic and repeat the procedure with student B starting, and a third topic with student C speaking first.

Discussion topics

- Brains are more important than beauty.
- Computer games are good for the mind.
- Intelligence isn't the most important thing for success.
- Eating good food can keep the brain healthy.
- Brain-training exercises.
- The importance of sleep.
- Exercising improves your thinking skills.
- Can music improve your brain power?

MODEL LANGUAGE

Paraphrasing
In other words …
To put it another way …
That is …

Phrases with *there*
There is evidence that …
There have been …
There are many ways in which …

Asking for advice
What advice do you have for … ?
So what can we do to …?
What do you suggest for this?
Do you think we ought to …?
What should we do when …?

Giving advice
You should/ought to …
It might be a good idea to …

ACKNOWLEDGEMENTS

Author acknowledgements

Many thanks to Andrew Reid for his excellent feedback and editorial work. Special thanks to Kate Hansford at CUP for overseeing the project and for her patience and support. Thanks to Carmen Konzett for her love, friendship and for always being ready to discuss language teaching. Thanks also to Felix Konzett for all the smiles and laughter and to Connor and Lauren Burnett for the beautiful drawings that brighten up my study.

Matt Firth

Publisher acknowledgements

The publishers are extremely grateful to the following people and their students for reviewing and trialling this course during its development. The course has benefited hugely from your insightful comments, advice and feedback.

Mr M.K. Adjibade, King Saud University, Saudi Arabia; Canan Aktug, Bursa Technical University, Turkey; Olwyn Alexander, Heriot Watt University, UK; Harika Altug, Bogazici University, Turkey; Laila Al-Qadhi, Kuwait University, Kuwait; Tahani Al-Taha, University of Dubai, UAE; Valerie Anisy, Damman University, Saudi Arabia; Anwar Al-Fetlawi, University of Sharjah, UAE; Ozlem Atalay, Middle East Technical University, Turkey; Seda Merter Ataygul, Bursa Technical University Turkey; Kwab Asare, University of Westminster, UK; Erdogan Bada, Cukurova University, Turkey; Cem Balcikanli, Gazi University, Turkey; Gaye Bayri, Anadolu University, Turkey; Meher Ben Lakhdar, Sohar University, Oman; Emma Biss, Girne American University, UK; Dogan Bulut, Meliksah University, Turkey; Sinem Bur, TED University, Turkey; Alison Chisholm, University of Sussex, UK; Dr. Panidnad Chulerk , Rangsit University, Thailand; Sedat Cilingir, Bilgi University, Istanbul, Turkey; Sarah Clark, Nottingham Trent International College, UK; Elaine Cockerham, Higher College of Technology, Muscat, Oman; Asli Derin, Bilgi University, Turkey; Steven Douglass, University of Sunderland, UK; Jacqueline Einer, Sabanci University, Turkey; Basak Erel, Anadolu University, Turkey; Hande Lena Erol, Piri Reis Maritime University, Turkey; Gulseren Eyuboglu, Ozyegin University, Turkey; Sam Fenwick, Sohar University, Oman; Peter Frey, International House, Doha, Qatar; Muge Gencer, Kemerburgaz University, Turkey; Dr. Majid Gharawi and colleagues at the English Language Centre, Jazan University, Saudi Arabia; Jeff Gibbons, King Fahed University of Petroleum and Minerals, Saudi Arabia; Maxine Gilway, Bristol University, UK; Dr Christina Gitsaki, HCT, Dubai Men's College, UAE; Neil Harris, Swansea University, UK; Vicki Hayden, College of the North Atlantic, Qatar; Joud Jabri-Pickett, United Arab Emirates University, Al Ain, UAE; Ajarn Naratip Sharp Jindapitak, Prince of Songkla University, Hatyai, Thailand; Aysel Kilic, Anadolu University, Turkey; Ali Kimav, Anadolu University, Turkey; Bahar Kiziltunali, Izmir University of Economics, Turkey; Kamil Koc, Ozel Kasimoglu Coskun Lisesi, Turkey; Ipek Korman-Tezcan, Yeditepe University, Turkey; Philip Lodge, Dubai Men's College, UAE; Iain Mackie, Al Rowdah University, Abu Dhabi, UAE; Katherine Mansfield, University of Westminster, UK; Kassim Mastan, King Saud University, Saudi Arabia; Elspeth McConnell, Newham College, UK; Lauriel Mehdi, American University of Sharjah, UAE; Dorando Mirkin-Dick, Bell International Institute, UK; Dr Sita Musigrungsi, Prince of Songkla University, Hatyai, Thailand; Mark Neville, Al Hosn University, Abu Dhabi, UAE; Shirley Norton, London School of English, UK; James Openshaw, British Study Centres, UK; Hale Ottolini, Mugla Sitki Kocman University, Turkey; David Palmer, University of Dubai, UAE; Michael Pazinas, United Arab Emirates University, UAE; Troy Priest, Zayed University, UAE; Alison Ramage Patterson, Jeddah, Saudi Arabia; Paul Rogers, Qatar Skills Academy, Qatar; Josh Round, Saint George International, UK; Harika Saglicak, Bogazici University, Turkey; Asli Saracoglu, Isik University, Turkey;

Neil Sarkar, Ealing, Hammersmith and West London College, UK; Nancy Shepherd, Bahrain University, Bahrain; Jonathan Smith, Sabanci University, Turkey; Peter Smith, United Arab Emirates University, UAE; Adem Soruc, Fatih University Istanbul, Turkey; Dr Peter Stanfield, HCT, Madinat Zayed & Ruwais Colleges, UAE; Maria Agata Szczerbik, United Arab Emirates University, Al Ain, UAE; Burcu Tezcan-Unal, Bilgi University, Turkey; Scott Thornbury, The New School, New York, USA; Dr Nakonthep Tipayasuparat, Rangsit University, Thailand; Susan Toth, HCT, Dubai Men's Campus, Dubai, UAE; Melin Unal, Ege University, Izmir, Turkey; Aylin Unaldi, Bogaziçi University, Turkey; Colleen Wackrow, Princess Nourah bint Abdulrahman University, Riyadh, Saudi Arabia; Gordon Watts, Study Group, Brighton UK; Po Leng Wendelkin, INTO at University of East Anglia, UK; Halime Yildiz, Bilkent University, Ankara, Turkey; Ferhat Yilmaz, Kahramanmaras Sutcu Imam University, Turkey.

Special thanks to Peter Lucantoni for sharing his expertise, both pedagogical and cultural.

Special thanks also to Michael Pazinas for writing the Research projects which feature at the end of every unit. Michael has first-hand experience of teaching in and developing materials for the paperless classroom. He has worked in Greece, the Middle East and the UK. Prior to his current position as Curriculum and Assessment Coordinator for the Foundation Program at the United Arab Emirates University he was an English teacher for the British Council, the University of Exeter and several private language institutes. Michael is also a graphic designer, involved in instructional design and educational eBook development. His main interests lie in using mobile technology together with attractive visual design, animation and interactivity. He is an advocate of challenge-based language learning.

Text and Photo acknowledgements

The authors and publishers acknowledge the following sources of copyright material and are grateful for the permissions granted. While every effort has been made, it has not always been possible to identify the sources of all the material used, or to trace all copyright holders. If any omissions are brought to our notice, we will be happy to include the appropriate acknowledgements on reprinting.

p.8:(1) © Eric Limon/Shutterstock; p.8: (2) © szefai/Shutterstock; p.8: (3) © Steven Vidler/Eurasia Press/Corbis.

All video stills by kind permission of © Discovery Communication, LLC 2014

Dictionary

Cambridge dictionaries are the world's most widely used dictionaries for learners of English. Available at three levels (Cambridge Essential English Dictionary, Cambridge Learner's Dictionary and Cambridge Advanced Learner's Dictionary), they provide easy-to-understand definitions, example sentences, and help in avoiding typical mistakes. The dictionaries are also available online at dictionary.cambridge.org. © Cambridge University Press, reproduced with permission.

Corpus

Development of this publication has made use of the Cambridge English Corpus (CEC). The CEC is a multi-billion word computer database of contemporary spoken and written English. It includes British English, American English and other varieties of English. It also includes the Cambridge Learner Corpus, developed in collaboration with Cambridge English Language Assessment. Cambridge University Press has built up the CEC to provide evidence about language use that helps to produce better language teaching materials.

Typeset by Integra.